Brick by Brick

Architecture and Interiors Built with Bricks

gestalten

An Introduction to the Prolific Use of Brick in Architecture

Brick is an incredibly versatile medium that lends itself to both solid sculptural forms and semitransparent screens.

The ancient practice of brickmaking has survived and evolved without ever losing the intrinsic nature of the brick itself. The brick's varieties are endless: we find blue bricks in China, terra-cotta in Italy, adobe in New Mexico, rammed earth in Niger, multihued clay bricks in Denmark, and cobogó cinder blocks in Brazil. Differing in shape, color, and technology, bricks are nonetheless universal and always reliable.

Embracing context, history, and masonry practices, brickwork is adaptable in tropical climates and in places where temperatures fluctuate incessantly. The earthy material responds and adapts to keep the hearth warm in Nordic homes and to absorb heat from the scorching sun in Southeast Asia.

Architect Louis Kahn used to say that decisions in architecture and construction were often prompted by the brick's response to what it wants to be. "You say to a brick, 'What do you want, brick?' And brick says to you, 'I like an arch.' And you say to brick, 'Look, I want one, too, but arches are expensive and I can use a concrete lintel.' And then you say: 'What do you think of that, brick?' Brick says: 'I like an arch.'" This leniency is important, as we must respect the nature of the most humble of construction materials.

Yet it is also the nature of the brick to allow for multiple pairings. Used along with timber, metal, or concrete, brick is never opposed to sharing the credit in a design. Which is not to say that brick needs the extra support—one of the most outstanding examples of its use is the thin-tile Catalan vault, which can be shaped symmetrically or can expand organically in different directions as in the Maya Somaiya Library by Sameep Padora & Associates in Kopargaon, India.

Brick also has the distinctive quality of unifying spaces and wrapping around buildings in more ways than one. Consider the dark-gray brickwork, draped like fabric, that envelops the MU:M office building by Wise Architecture in Paju-si South Korea or London's Brick Veil mosque by Luca Poian Forms, which references moucharaby lattice windows.

The brick's use in artistic interventions can be seen to render a sort of fantastic and not necessarily functional architecture, as in the pavilions of Per Kirkeby or photographer Filip Dujardin's quirky brick sculptures and labyrinthine dreamscapes. In Mile City, China, Cheng Chung Design's cave-like 50 percent Cloud Artists Lounge sits within an art installation by local artist Luo Xu. Known as Aboriginal Nest, the work takes shape as a cluster of skylit brick mounds resembling termite nests. Whether standing as a symbol for democracy as in Louis Kahn's National Assembly Building in Dhaka, completed in 1983, or as the utmost example of the prairie-style homes of Frank Lloyd Wright, Wingspread, from 1937, experiments in geometric plans and volumes also result in endless possibilities.

Elsewhere, historic mosques and cathedrals have paved the way for contemporary places of worship that honor the nature of the brick without the need for embellishment. Such is the case of the expansive Mayor Mohammad Hanif Jame Mosque in Dhaka, Bangladesh, by Shatotto, inspired by the pre-Mughal mosques, the open cylinder plan of the Slovenian Don Bosco Church chapel by Ljubljana-based DANS Architects, or the somewhat concealed Suzhou Chapel by Neri&Hu in Jiangsu.

Whether structural or applied as preformed panels, brickwork is unrivaled in bringing geometric uniformity to a facade.

Vernacular architecture also plays an important role in dictating the appropriate use for brick. The Three Courtyard Community Center built in Yangzhou, China by AZL Atelier Zhanglei, for example, looks to capture the typology of the neighboring structures. By simply continuing the roof profiles and using the local red terra-cotta bricks, the architects were able to contribute to, and revive, ancient practices that will withstand the test of time thanks to the implementation of modern technologies. It is interesting to note that, being readily available and sustainable, brick's solutions for shelter often take on similar aesthetic forms in different parts of the world, as in the use of barrel vaults and lattice screens at Intermediate House in Asunción, Paraguay by Equipo de Arquitectura or the Centro Multimedia Hñähñu by Aldana Sanchez in a rural municipality of Hidalgo, Mexico.

Beatty Vermeiren's Pattern House in Cape Town, South Africa, demonstrates just one of the countless ways of making brickwork a feature of a home's interior design.

Learning from our past—and especially from brickmakers who draw on tradition—is the best way to pay tribute and respect to the ancient practice of laying bricks. Pirouette House in Trivandrum, India, for example, uses a masonry method that stands bricks vertically, rather than laying them flat, facilitating cross ventilation. This innovative design of dancing walls by Wallmakers was aided by the expertise of local masons.

Showcasing 42 contemporary works, and examining their historic counterparts and references, this book highlights some of the best examples in the practice of brick architecture with a focus on interiors today. Considering aspects of history, technology, aesthetics, and sustainability, *Brick By Brick* offers a substantive guide for the continued use and innovation of the ancient material that keeps on giving.

Brick Techniques: Historical and Contemporary Craftsmanship

Bricks are ancient crafted materials that predate history. Immerse yourself into the process with the A–Z of bricks craftsmanship.

(Opposite) Songyue Pagoda. (Above) Thin bricks alternate with wide bands of mortar to create a decorative arched design.

Barrel Vault

As the name implies, this structure resembles the inside of a barrel. Also known as a tunnel vault, it is a semicylindrical form that makes up a continuous arched shape. Barrel vaults were utilized by ancient civilizations, such as the ancient Egyptians and Mesopotamians.

Bonding

The way bricks are arranged and laid in a construction. A "stretcher" bond is perhaps the simplest and most common form; bricks are laid lengthwise along the wall, alternating on each course. A "common" bond sees bricks laid lengthwise, like the stretcher bond, but with header layers—that is, with the bricks end on for every sixth course or row. A "Flemish" bond alternates between stretcher and header orientations across each course. These are just a few of the most common bonds, but a variety of others are prominent, including the "English cross" or "Dutch" bond, the "garden wall" bond, and the "soldier course."

Bricklayer

A tradesperson who lays bricks. A bricklayer is not a stonemason, as masons are involved in the cutting and shaping of stones, as well as in laying stones, bricks, and cinder blocks. As some of the world's oldest trades, bricklayers and masons have required multiple-year apprenticeships and on-site training since the earliest recordings of the profession.

Clay Brick

A type of masonry that is fired in a kiln at high temperatures to harden it. Clay bricks are dense and stronger than concrete bricks, making them suitable for both durability and insulation. They can be recycled at the end of their life cycle, which makes them a sustainable option, too. Once fired, bricks made from a metal-containing clay turn into a strong and heat-resistant ceramic-like material. Fired bricks that date as far back as 3000 BCE have been discovered in Rajasthan, India.

Course

A continuous row of bricks or masonry and mortar once constructed. Brick coursing charts are used to help bricklayers determine the number of bricks they will need to achieve a structure.

Dried Brick

The earliest form of brick, created by hardening clay earth or mud in the sun until it becomes hard enough to use in construction. The oldest dried bricks discovered date back to before 7500 BCE from an area close to Diyarbakır, Turkey. Sun-dried bricks such as mudbricks and adobe bricks are still used today and are seen as a sustainable yet labor intensive form of masonry.

Earth Brick

A brick that can be made from practically any ground that has clay-like features. Earth bricks are generally locally sourced and made. The material's ability to be locally sourced means that it avoids the heavy carbon emissions that accompany materials that need to be transported long distances. Alongside this, these bricks are generally composed of naturally derived materials, allowing them to have the potential to fully return to nature, meaning earth bricks are a highly sustainable option.

Frank Lloyd Wright worked with bricks on several of his domestic dwellings, using them to emphasize the linear forms he created.

Mariam Karama is known for applying modern technology to help preserve local, traditional building materials and techniques.

Frank Lloyd Wright

A pioneer of what he called "organic architecture," Frank Lloyd Wright made brick a feature of many of his iconic houses, alongside concrete, steel, and glass. He often used Roman brick to accentuate the long, horizontal lines of his structures, as seen in Robie House. Wright's brick homes are some of the United States' most iconic residential structures of the 20th century.

Grout

Generally a mix of water, cement, and sand, grout is most commonly used for tiling but is also used to embed rebar (reinforcement steel) into masonry. Grout is less firm than mortar and can also be used to fill the cores of concrete blocks.

Mariam Kamara

Mariam Kamara is an architect from Niger who is guided by the concept that architecture has the power to improve the quality of life of its users. Kamara focuses on materials that can be produced locally in African communities and that consider thermal comfort, social equity, and economic barriers. This focus on materiality and sustainability was partially influenced by Kamara's upbringing in the desert. Since founding her architecture and design studio, atelier masōmī in 2014 in Niger, her work has expanded globally.

Masonry

The process of building a structure using bricks, stone, or concrete blocks, using mortar as the binding material. The bricks or blocks used in the construction are themselves also referred to as masonry.

Mortar

A paste that hardens to ensure that bricks adhere to one another. Mortar's purpose is manifold. It is the bed and binding material of brick and blockwork, acting to fill gaps between the masonry and ensuring that the weight is evenly distributed. Typical mortars are composed of sand, water, and a binding element such as cement. Other constituents may include lime, bitumen, or even latex, which improves the strength and flexibility of the bond. While mortar is generally purely for structural purposes, its aesthetic properties are also sometimes taken advantage of, with cosmetic mortar adding colors or patterns.

Orientation

In masonry, this is the side and direction that a brick is facing. Each orientation has a different name: when a brick is laid perpendicular to the wall to expose its end and smallest side, it is called a brick "header." Laying all the bricks as headers creates a header or heading course. "Stretcher" refers to a brick that is laid horizontally with its long narrow side exposed. Stretchers are the only visible side in stretcher bonds and stack bonds. "Soldiers" are bricks laid vertically to display their long narrow side, as if standing side by side.

Perforated bricks have become a mainstay of sustainable architecture. Often locally sourced, they allow natural light and ventilation to permeate interior spaces.

One of the leading industrial designers of the early 20th century, Peter Behrens was a master of using brickwork on an unprecedented scale.

"Sailors" are bricks laid vertically with the broad face of the brick exposed, a feature most commonly used in decorative course ends.

Perforated Brick

A brick in which larger holes make up more than 25 percent of its volume is known as a perforated brick. These perforations generally mean the bricks use less energy for drying and firing and are also lighter and easier to handle, but they are sometimes also used for their decorative qualities. Perforated bricks are generally hard and dense, with a consistent shape and size.

Peter Behrens

A German architect known for his career in object, typeface, and building design, Peter Behrens began experimenting with brick expressionism after the First World War. His career in expressionism embraced lively ornamentation and color to develop buildings such as the iconic Hoechst Administration Building near Frankfurt, which has become one of Germany's foremost examples of the style.

Recycled Brick

A unit of masonry that is reused or repurposed at the end of its life cycle. There are two forms: the first is a brick that has come from a former project and is reused in a new project, often for its rustic aesthetic value or sustainable properties. The second form is a recycled brick that can be ground into aggregate and reformed into new bricks. Recycled bricks are often cheaper than new bricks and reduce carbon emissions and landfill.

Roman Brick

Referring to the bricks used in ancient Roman architecture as well as a style of brick popularized since the twentieth century, a Roman brick is characterized by its long, thin appearance. The Romans began using kilns to fire their bricks under Emperor Caesar Augustus. The process made brick production faster and the bricks stronger. This led to an increase in iconic public brick buildings, such as the Red Basilica in Pergamon.

Songyue Pagoda

One of the oldest-known standing brick buildings, dating back to 523 CE, the Songyue Pagoda is located on Mount Song in China. It stands at 130 feet (40 meters) high and is constructed from yellow brick and clay mortar.

Trowel

A tool with a pointed end, used for "buttering" mortar onto masonry. There is a range of trowels that can be used for different purposes. Pointing trowels, for example, allow bricklayers to shape the mortar between bricks, while bucket trowels are used to scoop mortar out of buckets and onto the masonry.

An example of a Roman barrel vault with decorative coffered details, dating from around 310 CE, at the Basilica of Maxentius in Rome.

Shaping Our Landscape with Bricks through the Ages

Brick—Our Constant Companion Throughout the Ages, From the Dawn of Civilization Through the Industrial Revolution and Into the Future

Adobe mudbricks remain the building material of choice for domestic architecture in the villages of the Sacred Valley, Peru.

Humans have long looked to their immediate environment for materials with which to build their dwellings. The first bricks were made in warm, dry climates by mixing earth with water, hand-shaping the mass into a practical, loaflike forms, and leaving them outside to harden under the sun. The oldest hand-formed mudbricks discovered by archaeologists, found in the Jordan Valley, are thought to be around 10,000 years old. This basic mudbrick technique is also known by the adopted Spanish term, *adobe*, whose roots reach back some 4,000 years, derived from the Arabic *aṭ-ṭūb*, and, before that, the Coptic *tōbe* and the Egyptian *ḏbt* (anglicization: *djebet*)—all meaning "brick."

A major milestone in the development of earthen bricks was the use of a straight-sided wooden mold—having uniform sizes and straight lines led to more rectangular structures overall. The earliest known molded mudbricks date to around 5000 BCE and were found in southern Mesopotamia (now Iraq). Mudbricks were also used in other river valley civilizations in the Middle East as well as in Africa, Asia, and South America.

Chan Chan, in northwestern Peru (c. 850 CE), was the largest known mudbrick city in the Americas. Its nine walled citadels included temples, homes, and storage buildings, some adorned with elaborate friezes—most of which have washed away over time.

The Great Mosque in Djenné, Mali (1907), is the largest existing mudbrick structure still standing today. The prayer hall can fit as many as 3,000 people, and the central tower is nearly 50 feet (15 meters) tall. It was built with hand-shaped cylindrical *Djenné ferey* mudbricks, made until the 1930s using a local technique. Later, rectangular *tubaabu ferey* (white-man's bricks) were adopted through the French colonists. Bundles of palm wood decorating the facade double as a scaffolding to aid repairs. To prevent damage from the seasonal floods, the mosque sits on a platform elevated nearly 10 feet (about 3 meters) above the ground. Due to the bricks' susceptibility to the rain and sun, the mosque must be replastered annually.

A major milestone in the development of earthen bricks was the use of a straight-sided wooden mold—having uniform sizes and straight lines led to more rectangular structures overall.

The invention of fired bricks was another breakthrough in brickmaking: when air-dried mudbricks are exposed to intense heat, they become significantly harder and longer lasting. This new technology enabled the production of bricks in cooler climates, where baking the bricks in the sun was not an option. The first fired bricks date to around 3500 BCE. Due to the labor and fuel costs of this further step in production, bricks were initially reserved for structures subject to greater wear, such as pavements, drains, or the tops of walls, and those with prestige, such as temples, tombs, and palaces. Over time, glazed brick was introduced; the Ishtar Gate of the Palace of Nebuchadnezzar in present-day Iraq (c. 575 BCE) was an artisanal feat in terms of molding and brickmaking. Walls were finished in glazed bricks mostly in blue, but also black, white, and gold, with animals and deities in low relief. One of the tallest and largest stupas of the ancient world was the Jetavanaramaya stupa, a Buddhist shrine in Anuradhapura, Sri Lanka (c. 273–301 CE). Built with some 93 million fired bricks and sealed with lime plaster, it was originally 400 feet (122 meters) tall, with a base area of 2,508,000 square feet (233,000 square meters).

Brick architecture spread throughout the Roman Empire (27 BCE–476 CE), thanks to the invention of portable kilns. Bricks were produced in various standardized shapes and sizes—round, square, oblong, and triangular—and used for buildings as well as for civil structures, such as aqueducts and bridges. As the Roman Empire declined in Western Europe, so did the prevalence of Roman brickwork and architectural forms. In Italy, the Byzantine Empire, and East Asia, brick architecture continued

Making mudbricks in Mali, West Africa. It is still traditional to make the bricks by hand, using a mold to achieve a uniform size.

to advance. Detailed descriptions of government standards for brick production, glazing, and bonding were included in the *Yingzao Fashi*, a technical treatise on architecture and craftsmanship written by the architect Li Jie and published in 1103 under the Song dynasty, which controlled most of present-day Eastern China.By the 14th century, a brick revival was underway in Northern and Central Europe, spurred on by the Hanseatic League maritime trade confederation and the close cultural exchange it promoted—not to mention the lack of stone and the copious quantities of clay in these areas. As fired bricks were still relatively expensive, their use was reserved for representative buildings. Gothic brick architecture is known for its decorative gables, glazed bricks, and elaborate rib vaults; custom-shaped bricks were used for a sculptural effect. The Copernicus House in the Hanseatic city of Toruń, Poland (15th century), is one such example. The combined warehouse and residence features an ornate brick facade with brick friezes and vertical recesses.

An impressive brick outlier during this period is Saint Basil's Cathedral on Moscow's Red Square (1555–61). Its eclectic blend of architectural influences includes Italian vaults, Islamic spires, and Muscovite ornamentation. The alluring novelty of brick can be seen in its widespread use for both structural and decorative purposes; stone walls inside are even painted to look like brickwork.

Throughout the 16th and 17th centuries, the Dutch were busy around the world—taking their bricks with them in the ships' hulls as ballast and export goods. Dutch brick traded widely to Scandinavia, England, the Channel Islands, and the Baltic region, where the small yellow vitrified *klinkers* became popular as a brick for paving. Dutch architecture was also introduced in the former colonies in Asia, Africa, the Caribbean, and America; Dutch settlers in New Amsterdam (now New York) were producing their own brick by 1628. In Potsdam, Germany, so keen was King Frederick William I to enlist the services of Dutch craftsmen to help build his city, that he invited native architect Jan Bouman to design living quarters for them. Still standing today, the 134 redbrick buildings of Potsdam's Dutch Quarter (1733–40) epitomize architecture seen in the Netherlands at the time.

The industrial revolution of the late 19th century heralded a new brick era, as machines and automation enabled mass production. The construction of factories, railroads, and other civil infrastructure greatly increased the demand for bricks. More precise molding and burning, and better access to different clays, increased the diversity of bricks available to meet functional and aesthetic demands. Early modernist architects embraced the new possibilities offered by mass production and explored the inherent qualities of building materials in their designs. While some rejected brick for its ties to the past, others delved into its potential for expression. Grundtvig's Church in Copenhagen, Denmark (1921–40), is a stunning synthesis of styles merging the pointed arches and ribbed vaults of classical Gothic architecture with the stepped gables of Danish vernacular and the modern geometries of brick expressionism. Designed by Peder Vilhelm Jensen-Klint, it was built with six million pale yellow bricks made from Danish clay.

Alvar Aalto's Experimental House in Muuratsalo, Finland (1952–54), delves into the possibilities offered by brick. Inspired by the idea of an ancient Roman atrium, the architect / designer's studio and summer house is made of 50 different types of fired clay brick, arranged in unique patterns. Situated in a coastal forest, it was also a study of how nature and the built environment interact.

Today, brick finds use in architecture in myriad ways around the world, existing comfortably alongside other construction techniques. It has been a constant companion throughout the ages and certainly seems destined to remain so for centuries to come.

The ancient adobe city of Chan, Peru, measured some 13 sq km (9 sq mi). Among its warren of streets, some walls were 9 m (30 ft) high.

Po Pagoda (977 CE) in Kaifeng, Henan Province, China, is made of more than 10,000 bricks featuring statues of Buddha.

Even at its current eroded height of 70.4 m (231 ft), Jetavanaramaya is the tallest remaining stupa (Buddhist shrine) from the ancient world.

Ancient Babylon's Ishtar Gate rose up 12 m (38 ft). Through it ran a brick-paved avenue that stretched more than ¾ km (½ mi) in length.

The bases of brick pillars at Pompeii, Italy. The fluting was likely carved or chipped away in situ before being coated in stucco.

The 15th-century Copernicus House in Torún, Poland, with its stepped gable and elaborate brickwork and tracery facade.

At Sanssouci, Potsdam, the redbrick walls of the Neues Palais proved so labor intensive and costly that Friedrich II had most of the palace rendered and painted to look like brick.

The arresting expressionist facade of Peder Vilhelm Jensen-Klint's Grundtvig's Church in Copenhagen, Denmark.

The 134 redbrick buildings that make up the historic Dutch Quarter of Potsdam are arranged on four main squares.

By the 14th century, a brick revival was underway in northern and central Europe, spurred on by the Hanseatic League maritime trade confederation and the close cultural exchange it promoted.

Anchor Mill, Paisley, Scotland. During the Industrial Revolution, numerous large-scale redbrick factories took shape in northern England and Scotland.

The eclectic, colorful St. Basil's Cathedral in Moscow, Russia. A one-off design, it has become a national icon.

Renovating and Restoring a Former Convent

Architects dmvA have created this site, known as Site Apostolinnen, by taking what was a convent before the 20th century and dividing it into a series of spaces that combine new buildings as well as the renovation and restoration of old ones. To reference the historic medieval lanes and alleyways once common in this region, the architects cleaned out the inner area of the site, displaying each historic volume individually while also creating new outdoor spaces. The Somerhuys (Summer House) at the heart of the site dates from the 17th century and has been restored for use as a private home. Behind it, a former worker's house has also been restored and renovated as eight student lodgings. One side of the site fronts the historic street Onze-Lieve-Vrouwestraat. Here, commercial spaces from the 19th century line the first floor, with six new residential units installed above and behind. Also on the site stands an entirely new building containing two triplex houses constructed from distinctive red bricks. Uniquely, the mortar oozes from between the masonry, adding a sculptural element to this historic site.

DMVA

SITE APOSTOLINNEN

MECHELEN, BELGIUM

(Above and opposite) Glimpses of the new brick building on the site, with its oozing mortar. Radiating out from the building, and enveloping the renovated Somerhuys at the heart of the development, a series of courtyards and alleyways provide circulation within the complex. (Previous page) External staircases create split-levels here and there, and a number of small patios.

Peckham's Angular, Sustainable Apartments

TIKARI WORKS

THE RYE

PECKHAM,
LONDON, U.K.

Occupying a corner across from Peckham Rye Park, The Rye rises up in an unusual angular form. The ground section of the building is a simple cement facade. Above, layers of red masonry shingles by Petersen Tegl emerge, interspersed with rectangular and square windows. The facade shifts partway up the third floor, where it leans backward, introducing a sloping surface that looks optimistically skyward. Windows across the building's facade act to give the building a unique identity with their irregular placement and ability to bend across eave levels. Inside, the large windows let in copious light, illuminating an interior that is kitted out with pale cross-laminated timber and apricot-and-white terrazzo floors. The building, which replaced a dilapidated, two-story postwar apartment block, was designed by Tikari Works, which acted as architect, developer, and main contractor, allowing the company to question the metrics-driven housing development model in favor of a high-quality, sustainable and sculptural form. Sustainability was integrated into the core of the design: the red shingles are dry-fixed and demountable, meaning they can be recycled at the end of their life cycle, passive energy-saving strategies are used throughout, and the cross-laminated timber frame is an incredibly efficient material for both embodied energy and cost.

114

(Opposite and previous pages) At street level, the Rye's two geometric volumes are unified by the concrete plinth on which they stand. The handmade Petersen Tegl shingles—all 10,000 of them—echo the red bricks of The Rye's Victorian neighbors, while the expansive windows afford generous views. (Right) Inside the apartments, cross-laminated timber lines not only the walls but also the ceilings.

A Staggered, Fanning Facade in Münster's Center

Despite its outline, which reflects the typical shape of a historic, pitch-roofed German home, the facade of Haus am Buddenturm emerges at unorthodox angles. Notably, it is staggered, with each level fanning out to gain maximum natural light through glazed sections in the eave walls and roof. The home is constructed from an array of thin, deep-red and brown mottled bricks. The bricks were hand-molded and fired in a ring kiln, the historic production method linking the structure to its heritage surroundings in the center of Münster. The facade has an opening on each level. On the first floor, a copper garage door is embellished with black lines, at once contrasting with the historic surroundings and repeating the angular aspects of the facade above. The second and third floors have larger windows than those in the surrounding houses, affording views of the medieval Buddenturm. The staggering of the front of the house is visible from the interior as well, where the bricks give way to untreated concrete and pale floorboards laid on sleepers.

HEHNPOHL ARCHITEKTUR BDA

HAUS AM BUDDENTURM

MÜNSTER, NORTH RHINE-WESTPHALIA, GERMANY

GRAZIA

(Opposite) Behind its almost traditional, mottled brickwork facade, Haus am Buddenturm is arranged on four floors, with rooms fanning out from the stairwell area. (Previous pages) At the rear of the building, full-width glazing presents an altogether more contemporary facade—its large windows flooding the voluminous, concrete- and wood-lined interior spaces with natural light.

A Soft Modern Hue Contrasts Old and New

With a considered and simple palette of handmade brick, concrete, and oak, Magri Williams has developed a humble yet sleek extension for this North London home. The historic nature of the location, a conservation area, gave the architects a starting point and informed their design choices. They developed an extension that follows the rear profile of the existing building and the angles of its roof. It takes shape as two pitched volumes that meet at a staggered point and slightly off-center. The handmade bricks were chosen with the "sensitive nature of the context" in mind, so as not to compete with the heritage area. A slightly imperfect tonal and textural variation in the new bricks echoes the time-worn characteristics, texture, and scale of the home's original bricks, yet subtly delineates the old from the new through their difference in hue. Inside the extension, the material palette is finite and meticulously chosen to reiterate the tonality of the brick, while maintaining a warmth. A beige concrete floor extends into the garden and is complemented by a bespoke oak kitchen, which is finished with a light whitewash.

MAGRI WILLIAMS

ALBERT ROAD

NORTH LONDON, U.K.

A Window Over Langhe Embedded in the Landscape

A large, painted-iron "portal" acts as a doorway to this property, visually framing both the spectacular vistas and the home itself, while imbuing a sense of artistry to the site. Surrounded by the rolling green hills of Langhe in Piedmont, Italy, Studioata's brickwork *Una Finestra sulle Langhe* is a patchwork of red, cream, and brown tones, aesthetically reflecting the nearby medieval castle of Cigliè. Inspired by views over the town of Mondovì, the Alpine arc, and the region's vineyards, nuts, and hazel trees, the architects have embedded the house within the landscape, while making the most of its views. The entire exterior is made from 21,500 Linea Terrae Bespoke Blend bricks, including the sloping roof, the chimneys, and a truncated cone skylight that protrudes at an angle to cast moving shadows across the building's surface. Stunning views pervade the interior; the front facade opens completely to provide sweeping views of the mountains through large glass panels, while a wall in the guest bedroom is punctuated by a Swiss-Cross motif, affording glimpses of Cigliè Castle.

STUDIOATA

UNA FINESTRA SULLE LANGHE

PIEDMONT, ITALY

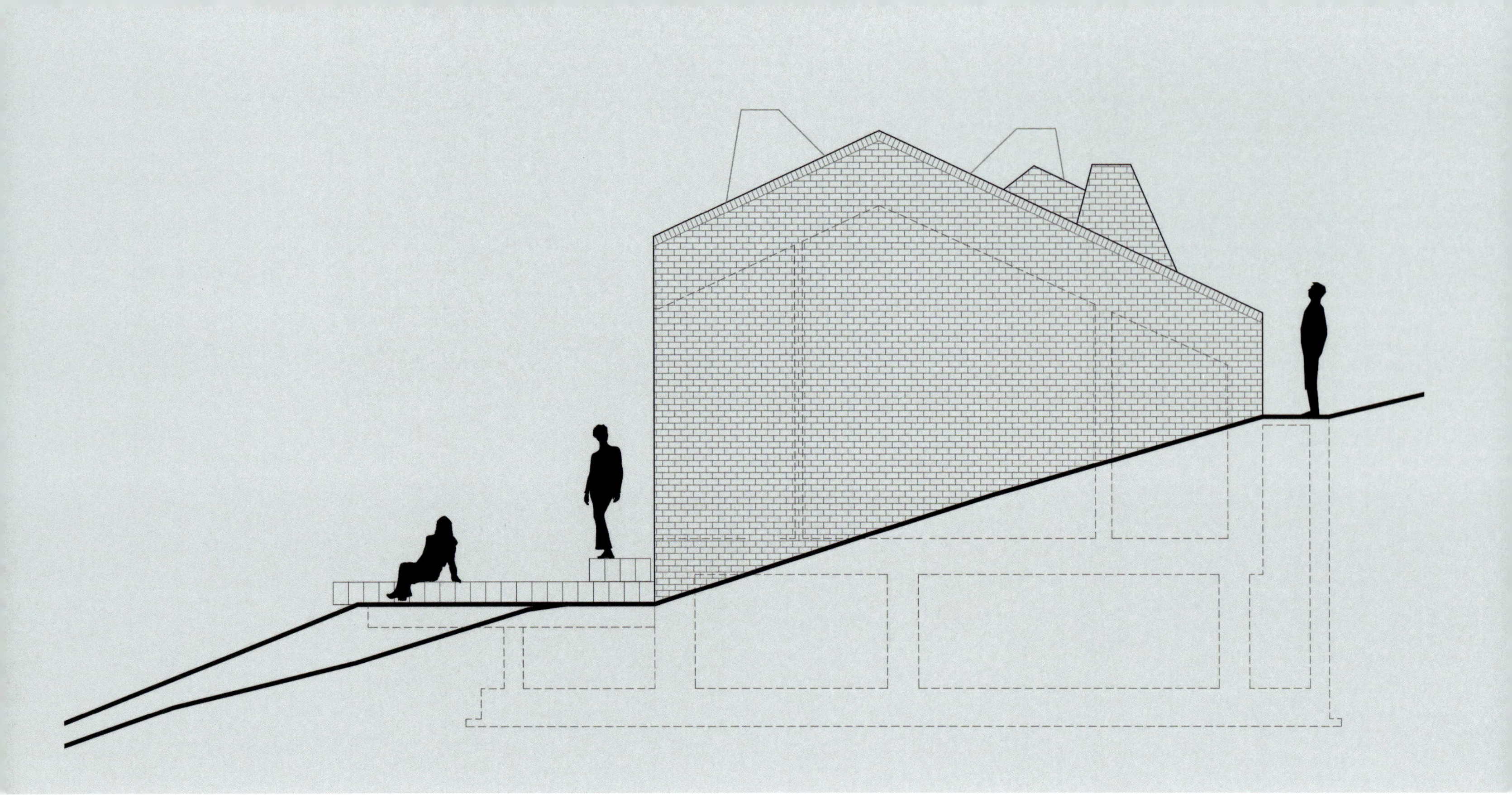

(Previous pages) Seen from the rear, the house is situated so unobtrusively within its steeply sloping site that it barely obstructs views of the stunning Italian countryside. (Opposite) Although a good portion of the building is embedded in the hillside, large windows to the front fill the rooms with light. (Above) From the glazed doors, a set of timber steps lead to a decked area outside.

An Earthy, Calming Extension

In a beachside suburb of Melbourne, Australia, architects at Studio Bright have added an extension to a sturdy postwar dwelling. Matching the original material, but diversifying the tone, the studio's gray-brick addition contrasts, yet complements, the traditional redbrick house. The original building was erected from clinker bricks, a type of brick that is formed from wet clay and exposed to excessive heat in the kiln in order to develop a shiny, dark coating. Referencing this historic material, Studio Bright selected ebony bricks by Adbri Masonry for their extension, achieving a cool and earthy inflection to the interiors. "Consisting of these dark bricks, the new volume gently touches the existing while establishing a new, contemporary architectural form and identity for the rear of the site," says Studio Bright. The sweeping, charcoal wall tones answer to the client's preference for a strong dark palette, and introduce a subtle character that enhances the solace of the space. Supplementary materials are minimal and the palette is restrained throughout. Black-stained timber lines the kitchen, while a gold island bench reflects sunlight onto the charcoal walls. Plants bring life and color to the introspective home, and in the courtyard, they hang down through a circular Carlo Scarpa-esque opening in the overhead concrete roof.

STUDIO BRIGHT

CLINKER BRICK HOUSE

MENTONE, MELBOURNE, AUSTRALIA

(Opposite) Inside the house, the original, well-worn—once exterior—red-brick facade meets the clean lines of the gray-brick extension, while wood-strip flooring transitions to polished concrete floors. The lines mark the point at which old becomes new. (Left and below) Inside the extension, a selection of carefully curated furnishings blends in with the gray-brick walls.

A generous amount of natural light finds its way into the rooms of the house, mellowing the tones of the deliberately dark palette. At the rear of the house, the new gray-brick extension wraps around a small, sheltered garden that leads off several rooms of the house and features a black-tiled, partially covered terrace. Up above, a roof garden provides additional outside space.

Salvaged Bricks Contrast with Contemporary Fixtures

Inside Martin Skoček's House V, a pitched timber ceiling runs the length of the building, above recycled aged-brick walls. The combination has a somewhat church-like quality; the space feels as if it could once have been a rural place of worship. The home, however, is a modern rendition of typical rural development in Bratislava and stands on a site where a dilapidated building once stood. The former building was deconstructed brick by brick so that they could be reused anew and the character partially maintained. Softly contrasting with the historic salvaged bricks, contemporary fittings and fixtures abound and include a statement steel kitchen island that sits solidly below a row of spherical pendant lamps. One long wall of the living room and kitchen gives way to large, black steel-framed glass windows and sliding doors that open onto a grassy garden, a pool, and a neighboring building with a charming vine-covered wall and traditionally shingled roof. The exterior of the home is simple. A gabled titanium zinc roof tops the house, contrasting with the exterior walls, which have been painted crisp white.

MARTIN SKOČEK

HOUSE V

BRATISLAVA, SLOVAKIA

(Previous pages) There is a stark contrast between the somewhat prosaic exterior of the house and its almost cathedral-like interiors, the salvaged bricks lending the spaces a warm, almost rustic character. Furnishings remain minimalist and contemporary, however, from the deep-sided freestanding bathtub in the bathroom to a low-slung bed overlooking the garden (opposite).

(Opposite) Beneath the double-height pitched-timber ceiling, and running parallel to the garden is a combined open-plan kitchen, dining room, and living room, fully glazed along one side. (Above) In the corridors between the main living spaces, clever storage solutions include ceiling-height cupboards with solid oak doors and a ladder for accessing those out-of-reach spaces.

Recycled Bricks Bring Variation and Texture

At the rear of Garden Wall House is an angular and lofty, gray-brown brick structure, its checkered face allowing light into the building and breaking up what would otherwise be a stark and imposing facade. The dark-brick wall is fashioned from Mowbray Blue Dry Pressed Architectural bricks by PGH Bricks, chosen by Studio Bright for their durable, textural properties. The bricks reference the historic context of the site, while also providing a privacy screen. With a site measuring just 15 feet (4.5 meters) wide, the architects found themselves playing a "game of millimeters," to ensure that this Melbourne residence maintained a feeling of spaciousness and calm. White-brick garden walls run uninterrupted into the house, bringing lightness inside. Made from recycled bricks for their subtle and imperfect variations, the white bricks provide a welcome texture to the otherwise minimal kitchen and living area. The light tone also works to visually enhance the size of the space, producing a serene and airy interior.

STUDIO BRIGHT

GARDEN WALL HOUSE

MELBOURNE, AUSTRALIA

Locally Handcrafted Bricks Foster Modern Serenity

Pale brick is paired with concrete, oak joinery, and quarry stones to bring natural warmth to this serene, contemporary home. Just northwest of Mexico City's metropolitan area, Casa Mika by Arquitectura Sergio Portillo features simple geometric lines, a nominal palette of finishes, and subtle vegetation. The white clay brick was locally handcrafted—an eco-conscious choice that also underlies the home's ethos—and was chosen for its sharp aesthetic, thermal comfort, and potential for textural variation. This last is evident in a courtyard where bricks cover two walls and the ground in a compact arrangement, while a third wall, with more sparsely spaced brickwork, provides a moment of respite. The whole structure is enlivened with greenery. In each exterior space, plants grow between cracks in the bricks, as if nature is subtly taking back the space. From inside, the living room and dining room look out through large, brick-framed sliding doors, onto a courtyard filled with trees and plants.

ARQUITECTURA SERGIO PORTILLO (ASP)

CASA MIKA

MEXICO CITY, MEXICO

A great deal of consideration has gone into the brickwork, both inside and outside of the building. Outside, crazy paving stones are juxtaposed with the neatly ordered external facades, where a change in direction of the bricks above the window introduces even more contrast; inside, a wall flooded with natural light features bricks that have been laid end-on to create texture.

Equal Parts Rustic Brick and Thick Mortar

The exterior of Malu de Miguel's MS5 in Boadilla del Monte is characterized by rustic, textured masonry that is divided by mortar equally as thick as the bricks it encases. The long, thin shape of the bricks is reminiscent of Roman masonry, yet the contrast of mortar, the pale terra-cotta color of the bricks, and the sleek shape of the home ultimately present a modern facade. Internally, a double-height living room creates a contemporary gallery-esque space. The bricks persist inside but, here, they're laid in stack bonds directly on top of each other, presenting purely an aesthetic rather than structural use. While this bond doesn't provide structural support, it is used decoratively as a shower recess, window frames, and shelves, giving an effective display of the brickwork's geometric charms alongside the uncharacteristically thick mortar. The interior brickwork is paired with concrete that has been imprinted with OSB board. The texturing, along with the complementary brickwork, creates a more organic and warm appearance.

MALU DE MIGUEL

MS5

BOADILLA DEL MONTE, MADRID, SPAIN

Presenting a neat single-story, windowless facade at street level, the house is in fact a bright, voluminous building with airy, double-height spaces. The use of brick and OSB-imprinted concrete has a striking effect here, lending the design a contemporary edge, yet with rough textures and dry, earthy tones that echo those of the home's immediate natural surroundings.

Brick for Building Less and Giving More

When the clients of Brick and Gable House first approached Breathe, they were looking for a larger home to house their family and to cater to their love of entertaining. But after a year overseas, they returned to Australia with renewed priorities, having realized the amount of space they needed to live comfortably was less than they originally thought. "We respected this decision tremendously, and we started schematic design over, with the brief and budget cut in half," said Breathe, an architectural practice that is renowned in Australia for its sustainable practices. The architects updated the kitchen, living room, and dining room to ensure the clients had space for entertaining. A freestanding brick studio was added as an extension to the back of the home, while the heritage-listed facade of the original Victorian brick terrace was retained, and minimal alterations made to the terrace itself. "The project prioritizes functionality, livability, and sustainability," says Breathe. As such, robust, sustainable materials—including recycled red bricks, Australian blackbutt timber veneer joinery, and recycled Tasmanian oak floorboards combine to offer a homey materiality. By using recycled bricks, Breathe was able to reduce the embodied energy of the project. Double-brick stack bond walls act as insulation, while also simplifying construction by reducing the need for other materials. All in all, the house admirably lives up to Breathe's motto to "build less, give more."

BREATHE

BRICK AND GABLE HOUSE

PORT MELBOURNE, VICTORIA, AUSTRALIA

Building the extension from scratch enabled the architects to use sustainable materials throughout. Coupled with the lean geometry of bespoke cabinetry and shelving, the recycled red bricks and wood finishes add warmth to the bright contemporary interior spaces. (Below) The once-exterior facade of the original house has been whitewashed to maintain the minimalist look.

The Home That Inspired a Movement

With its pitched, red-tiled roof and medieval and neo-Gothic inspired exterior, Red House is an iconic 19th-century British home, with a name inspired by its exposed brick exterior. Drawing on 13th-century British medieval influences, architect Philip Webb and designer William Morris conceived a unique design. Reflecting Morris's artisanal craftsmanship construction of the home, the building became a significant and early example of the Arts and Crafts Movement—a movement that reacted against a perceived decline in standards associated with post-industrial revolution factory production—of which Morris is often considered the founder. Another reason for the home's renown was its plain and severe exterior, which contrasted with the heavily ornamented facades of the time. Other unique touches include the fenestration, which disregards the home's exterior symmetry in favor of creating the best windows for each room. Unusually, the servants' quarters were larger than the standard, an indication of the designers' socialist ideologies. The masonry continues throughout the interior, with exposed-brick arches and fireplaces. Stained-glass windows, plastered walls and ceilings, and dark timber finishes are also markers of the interior.

PHILIP WEBB AND WILLIAM MORRIS

RED HOUSE

1860

LONDON, U.K.

A Reinvigorated Historic Paper Factory

An alluring history surrounds The Parchment Works by Will Gamble Architects, an extension built in the remnants of a 16th-century parchment paper factory. The ruin is composed of a patchwork of brick and stone and has been restored to retain structural integrity while keeping the charm of its semi-decayed state. Originally, the residents of the Victorian cottage on whose grounds the ruin stands, requested its demolition in order to make way for an extension. The architects instead suggested designing the extension within the ruin, in a bid to preserve the history of the site. Further, they chose bricks to feature throughout, so linking the old with the new. Sourced from a demolished building on the same site, the upcycled material proved both a cost-effective and a sustainable measure. An unostentatious combination of weathering steel and oak join the reclaimed brick on the building's facade, while, inside, the masonry is paired with a state-of-the-art kitchen and historic oak beams—a further amalgamation of the historic with the contemporary. What results is a celebration of the historic masonry building that harmonizes succinctly with the contemporary update and the Victorian-era cottage.

WILL GAMBLE ARCHITECTS

THE PARCHMENT WORKS

NORTHAMPTONSHIRE, U.K.

Combining recycled materials to create walls made variously from stone and brick, the architects have preserved the charming, ramshackle appearance of the original ruins. (Opposite and next pages) Taking a stepped form, the extension is cleverly absorbed within the crumbling walls of the original building. As such, it does not encroach on the visual impact of the ruins, but rather contributes to it.

Beyond Red: A Look at the Numerous Aesthetics of Brick

Shape, Size, and Color May Fluctuate, but Brick's Intrinsic Nature as a Material Derived from the Earth Is Universal

The curvaceous brick forms of Studio Zhu-Pei's Imperial Kiln Museum, Jingdezhen, China (opposite), and BLAF Architecten's g|G House (above).

While architectural work in wood, stone, and concrete will always remain adaptable and reliable, brickwork is the only material that will never cease to be considered craftsmanship. Multilayered and multicolored, with sharp or sinuous corners and arches, brick can be transformed and recontextualized over and over again according to its place and mode of use. Brick's engineering capabilities helped ancient civilizations build impressive structures such as the steep mudbrick Meroitic pyramids from the final period of the Kingdom of Kush in Northern Sudan and the monumental Roman Baths of Caracalla. Precisely because of their organic and malleable nature, clay bricks have the power to raise a building to the highest level of sophistication, but also to produce the most unassuming form of shelter. While it remains the most basic and humble of building materials, brick can be anything we want it to be—as long as we acknowledge "what the brick really wants," as the late architect Michael Sorkin wrote.

It may seem at first glance, as it is virtually omnipresent, that there must be a standard for the measurements of a single brick. Yet metrics apply in different countries that dictate the length, depth, and height of one modest clay brick. While in the United Kingdom the standard modern brick measures 8.5 × 4 × 2.5 inches (21.5 × 10.2 × 6.4 centimeters), India's typical brick measures 7.5 × 3.5 × 3.5 inches (19 × 9 × 9 centimeters), and the United States' widely used modular brick is 7.6 × 3.6 × 2.2 inches (19.3 × 9 × 5.7 centimeters).

While the cult of the brick is global, it has its own characteristic elements according to its source—the traditional gray brick ubiquitous in China or the multicolored earth bricks used in Denmark, for example. Whether it be made of red clay, rammed earth, or recycled material, brick can respond to both the architect's needs and the user's experience.

In the Binh Thanh district of Ho Chi Minh City, Vietnam, Sanuki Daisuke architects created a multipatterned cinder-block facade providing privacy, light, and ventilation.

The architect and critic Carlos Mijares Bracho, arguably Mexico's pioneer in experimental brick architecture, wrote "Brick is the first building material that can be called—strictly speaking—a prefabricated material." He continued, "With brick—earth, water, and fire—it is possible to make floors, walls, columns, pilasters, arches, lintels, and domes; but also steps, moldings, ornamental elements, textures, and diverse rhythms and rigging."

While it is eventually up to the artisan or the architectural designer to find the adequate fit for construction, one thing that remains common is the sourcing of the material. Places built along the banks of a river often rely on its mud as the base for creating a local clay for sun drying or firing as bricks. Examples include mud-and-straw bricks from the Nile region, used since ancient Egyptian civilizations, and the centuries-old traditional methods used in Taos, New Mexico, both of which help regulate increasingly extreme temperatures.

Every work of architecture made in brick corresponds—or should correspond—to the local climate, the history, and the people inhabiting or transitioning a space. Throughout the history of modern urbanization, residential buildings were widely constructed in brick. However, this was not always the case, as architect Francesca Torzo writes in her "Notes on cities and places. Copenhagen," where she speaks of the city's history of building with clay bricks stating that, at one point, after the massive fire of 1728, "wooden constructions were banned and brick became the reference material, even for private buildings." A similar argument was made by "the architect of New York" Rafael Guastavino, who, in the late 19th century, applied his signature thin-tiled Catalan vault to multiple buildings and stations all over the city under the patented argument that they would never catch fire.

While fire is always a concern, the main feature of these compression-only vaulted structures is their ability to span considerable distances without the need for further support by beams or columns. They provide visual continuity and harmony, while also creating phenomenal aural experiences.

An example of a residential architectural design planned around vaulted ceilings is the Vault House by South Korean studio OBBA. Its curved, redbrick walls wrap around a central barrel vault. Two main oval shapes intersect between open-air and indoor spaces, creating sweeping rooms in all directions with openings that frame the sky and the surrounding landscape.

A range of bricklaying techniques adds rich texture to the facades of Gallery House in West Bengal by the Abin Design Studio.

One of the most familiar forms of brickwork is the row house, found in London as the 17th-century townhouse; in Philadelphia, in the early-18th-century narrow alleyways only wide enough for a carriage; or in Brooklyn, New York, as the ubiquitous 19th-century brownstone. This typology of near-identical homes has withstood the test of time and continues to be widely sought after among city-center residents in metropolises worldwide, who seek small, open-plan, and primarily vertical spaces.

The adaptive reuse of old buildings and fitting new homes into vacant lots are challenges best faced when using brick. Studio Ben Allen, for example, known for its use of double-height vaulted ceilings, created an extension for the backyard of an existing Victorian house. Handmade York bricks make up and bear the weight of two barrel vaults that extend the kitchen and dining/study room, making way for natural light on both ends.

In other, not-so-narrow places where, nonetheless, houses are built one right next to the other in similar styles, it is interesting to find reinterpretations of traditional brick architecture. In Münster, Germany, the Haus am Buddenturm by hehnpohl architektur bda—somewhat reminiscent of Marcel Breuer's brutalist Whitney Museum in New York—contrasts with the city's classic aesthetic, keeping a respectful nod to the gable house profile.

Sinuous walls like those of the Baker House at MIT by Alvar Aalto are designed for acoustic purposes to lessen the outdoor traffic noise. Far from the city and in the woods, its contemporary counterpart could be the gjG house in Belgium by BLAF Architecten, which is made of reused bricks.

Cinder blocks—perforated bricks in an array of patterns—are prominent in regions with a tropical climate, such as Vietnam or Brazil, where the cobogó brick originated. Cities in Vietnam, where space is an issue, opt for narrow multi-story homes that make their way into tight lots. Here, solutions like cinder-block walls are essential.

Similarly, an entire building can be enveloped by a perforated screen allowing for sheltered balconies, while filtering sunlight and providing protection from the elements, as in the reticulated facades of the Bat Trang House by VTN Architects or the Brick Cave by H&P Architects, both in Hanoi. A residential building in the Rwanda neighborhood of Addis Ababa, Ethiopia, by New York firm AD-WO, is likewise comprised of a core building with a 6-foot (2-meter) offset surrounding brick wall bridged with plant-filled connecting balconies.

At Casa Joven in San Francisco, Argentina, the architects have used a perforated brick screen to distance the house from the street.

CAD-generated software now makes it possible to design textured and decorative walls like those of Admun Design & Construction Studio in Tehran or the "grapes" on the winery facade developed by Gramazio & Kohler in Fläsch, Switzerland, with ETH Zurich.

Zigzagged, curved, and stepped brickwork designs create rhythm and repetition, often with results that are aesthetically pleasing to the eye and the body in general. We seek places that bring us solace and ease, and we look for patterns and compositions that remind us of sequences we know from nature. What's more, the brick offers a direct connection to the earth itself and a sense of grounding.

As part of the regeneration of Site Apostolinnen in Mechelen, Belgium, architect dmvA mounted a skylight on a brickwork base.

A beautifully curved, whitewashed brickwork facade is the principal feature of an extension to Caroline House in Melbourne, Australia.

Petersen Tegl bricks are used to construct the irregular angular forms of two sister buildings at The Rye in Peckham, London.

The brick vaults at Studio Zhu-Pei's Imperial Kiln Museum, Jingdezhen, China, are based on the form of a traditional kiln.

At House DG in Belgium, Lens°ass architects have created a brickwork diamond mesh to shield the interior from direct sunlight.

The unconventional shape of the building adds to the textural intrigue of Gallery House in West Bengal, India.

Curved brickwork is a salient feature of GRAFT architect's remodeling of a decommissioned post office in Berlin, Germany.

There is a certain fluidity in the undulating brick-work walls and partitions that characterize Pirouette House in Kerala, India.

Zigzagged, curved, and stepped brickwork designs create rhythm and repetition, often with results that are aesthetically pleasing to the eye, and the body in general.

At Tate Modern, London, architects Herzog & de Meuron sought a modern brick to match that of the original building, a power station built in the 1940s.

For The Parchment Works, in Northamptonshire, U.K., Will Gamble Architects took pains to incorporate the decayed walls of ruins in the grounds.

An Undulating Emulation of Dance

WALLMAKERS

PIROUETTE HOUSE

TRIVANDRUM, KERALA, INDIA

The brick facade of Pirouette House in Trivandrum, Kerala, forms a twisting entity that emulates a twirling dancer—hence the dwelling's name. The material is used gracefully and placed at varying depths to create a kinetic and undulating surface that slants left and then right, converging to support the roof. The architects, Wallmakers, employed a brickwork technique known as rat trap bond masonry. Conceived by architect Laurie Baker of Kerala fame, the technique sees bricks placed vertically rather than the traditional horizontal alignment. This creates hollows in the wall, aiding thermal efficiency, but it also cuts down on the number of bricks needed. This is not the only exercise in minimal material use: recycled wood paneling makes up part of the flooring and the roof is made of ferro-cement shells. These wafer-like, steel-reinforced arched shells significantly reduce both cement and steel consumption. Meanwhile, brick is a feature not only of the exterior but also becomes an intrinsic characteristic of the interior. For example, in the master bedroom, the bricks form a structured and regular geometric pattern above the bed, while the facing wall replicates the smooth, waving qualities of the building's exterior.

Sustainability lies at the heart of this intriguing design. (Opposite and previous pages) Inside the house, the floor in the kitchen is largely made from recycled scaffold planks—some of them painted—that give way to polished concrete. (Below) Throughout the house are screens and furniture pieces that have been woven using locally sourced cane.

(Above) A metal screen flanks a staircase leading to the upper level—the open treads radiating out from a tree trunk. Both the screen and the stairs are constructed from the scaffold poles used in constructing the house. (Opposite, top) A kink in the wall provides an alcove for a built-in work surface. (Opposite, bottom) The full impact of the "pirouetting" walls on the building's facade.

Salvaged Tiles Lend a Quirky Yet Nostalgic Nod to the Past

In this Vietnamese property, fish-scale tiles salvaged from the plot's previous house are combined with red brickwork to create a facade that resembles the rippling skin of a sea creature. Peeking above the roofline of its neighbors, the skinny home's red aesthetic is unashamedly bold with a dash of eccentricity. The house occupies just half the site, leaving the rest of the land for gardening and entertaining—a welcome escape from the surrounding urban area and a space for the homeowners' children to play. The interior of the building is defined by a second level comprised of two volumes—one at each end of the long, skinny home. The balconies of each volume are surrounded by the unique fish-scale tiling and connected by a single, narrow walkway under a large, clear roof. The transparent roof lets a cool breeze in through vents, creating an atrium-like feeling and bringing copious light to the ground floor. The warm, red bricks of 2Hien are raw and simple, while the recycled tiles offer a nostalgic nod to the property's past.

CTA CREATIVE ARCHITECTS

2HIEN

BINH THANH DISTRICT, HO CHI MINH CITY, VIETNAM

(Page 86 and opposite) The high, windowless walls of the neighboring buildings help to create a tranquil, private garden at the street entrance to the plot. (Previous pages and above) At the center of the house, the glazed roof and bedroom balconies create an internal courtyard space that blurs the lines between inside and outside—an effect that is only emphasized by the fish-scale tiles.

A Punctured Facade Determines Privacy and Illumination

On the street, the facade of Casa Joven, or Young House, stands tall and certain against the boundary of its plot. The assertive wall is softened by regular perforations in the brickwork that make it a semi-sheer screen. This facade shelters the entrance courtyard and acts as a partition between the street noise and the home beyond, yet allows cross ventilation through the home when the sliding doors behind it are opened. Internally, these perforations limit the amount of intense afternoon sunlight entering through the tall sliding doors, while creating varying patterns and colors on the interior, depending on the sunset. Consequently, the punctured facade determines a perfect combination of privacy, illumination, and noise reduction. The Argentinian home was designed for a young man by 226 Arquitectos and is a simple studio-like abode with open-plan living and dining and a mezzanine bedroom. The brickwork continues inside, where it is paired with concrete slabs, simple cream tiles, and aluminum window frames. Bricks were chosen for their sturdiness against the locale's strong winds and minimal need for maintenance.

226 ARQUITECTOS

CASA JOVEN

SAN FRANCISCO, ARGENTINA

The front of the house is fully glazed, yet maintains maximum privacy from the street, thanks to the double-height perforated-brick facade. It is a design that allows for a permanent stream of dappled natural light to enter the home, sometimes made more diffuse via shades and blinds. (Above) Between the wall and the house is a narrow garden, also shaded by the perforated wall.

The Rustic and the Contemporary Merge Through Materiality

A selection of uncomplicated materials combine to create Casa 1219, a minimal yet welcoming residence in a small province of Barcelona, Spain. Rather than adopting lightweight construction materials, HARQUITECTES opted to use brick owing to the material's passive thermal properties, which help regulate temperature in this region's varying climate. To ensure integrity on the plot's low-resistance ground, the long and low rectangular shape of the house spreads the weight of its bricks via equidistant walls. On the exterior, the lower two-thirds of the home is composed of thick, pastoral terra-cotta bricks, while thinner bricks of the same color make up the upper third, giving the building a lighter appearance. Inside, the brickwork continues through the communal living and dining areas, where it is accompanied by cement floors and terra-cotta-colored ceramic ceiling tiles spanning the roof in gentle arcs. In the bedrooms, white walls and ceilings contrast with the rustic tiles and bricks, giving the suburban home a nuanced, contemporary feel.

HARQUITECTES

CASA 1219

PALAU-SOLITÀ I PLEGAMANS, BARCELONA, SPAIN

The design of this single-story house is based on a grid of 10 equal-sized units, configured to create a series of small, intimate rooms as well as a long open-plan living/dining space fronting the garden. (Above and opposite) Having equidistant walls means that all openings in the walls are the same size, whether leading from one room to the next inside the house, or out into the garden.

An Adaptable Brick Facade with a Focus on Sustainability

An unexpected garden tops the roof of AgriNesture, an otherwise simple, cuboid, brick structure. In Vietnam, a combination of rapid urbanization and significant population growth has drastically reduced agricultural land in the country, diminishing the contact between humans and nature. AgriNesture aims to bring back that connection by promoting agriculture, the house being a prototype for what could be a cluster of the houses that, together, create a sky-bound field on their roofs. Should the home be replicated, its structure can be adapted to suit any locale. The two-story building consists of a reinforced concrete frame covered in bricks, but its external material can be altered depending on the region's availability, increasing sustainability by reducing logistics. The roof is a place for agriculture, with a rainwater collection and recycling system used for watering the plants. While eco-conscious, the home's combination of exposed red bricks, cement, and steel, alongside pops of greenery, mindfully creates an effective aesthetic appeal.

H&P ARCHITECTS

AGRINESTURE

MẠO KHÊ, VIETNAM

(Previous pages) An otherwise uniform facade is interrupted by perforated sections of wall. (Above and opposite) Inside the house, an unconventional layout creates a mixture of single- and double-height spaces. It is a versatile design that allows a young tree to rise up through two floors of the building, and for a selection of plants to hang suspended above the first-floor living space.

ROSSI

A Rippling Facade Inspired by Terra-Cotta Temples

Contrasting depths and juxtapositions in the exposed brick masonry and ceramic walls of Gallery House by Abin Design Studio (ADS) characterize this energetic and artistic project. The rippling structure, located in Bansberia, a town almost 30 miles (48 kilometers) from Kolkata, India, is highly decorative, taking cues from Bengal's terra-cotta temples, yet distinctly modern when compared with neighboring structures. A closer look at the building reveals that each layer of bricks achieves a different purpose: one layer features gaps that allow light into the building, for example, while another serves as a decorative feature with a herringbone pattern. The combined brick and ceramic patterning reflects the mixed-use function of the building itself. Originally this site was destined to be a parking lot for the client's vehicles. With encouragement from ADS, however, the client agreed to extend the upper level to create a multipurpose space for the neighborhood. "Encouraged to maximize the public utility of this building, its design was conceived to extend into the street, both visually and physically," say ADS. On the facade, a tall, wide arch curves around one corner of the building to reveal a glimpse of the concrete interior, and presents the brick as a skin-like feature of the building. The project is inherently local, with the clay for the terra-cotta bricks sourced from the banks of a nearby river and a ceramic artist collaborating on the ceramic blocks. "These two were combined," says ADS, "using locally prevalent finesse of building masonry."

ABIN DESIGN STUDIO (ADS)

GALLERY HOUSE

BANSBERIA, WEST BENGAL, INDIA

The building's intricate brick and ceramic skin surrounds an inner concrete volume, creating an expansive public space that can be accessed from the street. (Opposite) In the corner above the entrance arch, a series of huge concrete slabs mark the exposed underside of a sweeping flight of stairs that leads to a terrace on the building's roof.

Two Perforated Brick Walls Blur Boundaries Between Inside and Out

A carefully constructed, perforated brick exterior creates an effective shield around this project, allowing light and airflow into the home's wrap-around courtyard, while maintaining the residents' privacy and reducing noise and harsh sun from the west. The skewed, somewhat trapezoidal shape of the exterior hides a second, interior, wall—also perforated. The exterior wall begins to angle inward at a height of around 6.5 feet (2 meters), meeting the interior wall at the top. A garden occupies the flat roof—a small hat of greenery that allows the plants to become intertwined with the fabric of the building. Balconies jut out from the interior structure into the atrium-like space between the two walls, blurring the idea of inside and out. Greenery is the focus here, too, with an abundance of plants bringing life to the building. Redefining the ideas around typical local brickwork, H&P Architects created this cave-like structure, exploring the function and potential of the material. Inside the home, timber, glass, and polished stone floors combine with the bricks to create a cooling yet homey space.

H&P ARCHITECTS

BRICK CAVE

ĐÔNG ANH, HANOI, VIETNAM

SONHA

(Previous pages) The combination of perforated brick and mesh sections in the walls of the building's interior and exterior facades allows for well illuminated and ventilated spaces between the two skins and within the house itself. (Page 110 and opposite) The design of the building ensures intriguing views—of inner courtyard spaces, the sky, strips of greenery—from almost every vantage point.

Snow Catching on a Sculptural Redbrick Facade

A barrel-vaulted ceiling is the focal point of Batay-Csorba Architects' High Park Residence. The curved feature runs down the right side of the ground floor, all the way from the street-facing entrance to the rear of the house. At the front, an adaptation of Flemish bond brickwork sees protruding bricks forge a geometric pattern across the tall facade. When it snows, small piles of white gather atop the brickwork headers, creating unexpected dashes of brightness across the otherwise dark bricks. The architects chose brick to tie in with the dominant fabric of the surrounding buildings, and as a nod to Toronto's historic use of brick since the first Victorian houses were built in the 19th century. Nevertheless, the design stands out as unexpectedly modern beside its pitch-roofed neighbors. In stark contrast to the dark, textured exterior, inside is minimal, bright, and brick free. A curved white ceiling highlights the continuous barrel vault, dispersing light and air through the house, while light timber floors and a cozy fireplace bring warmth to the home.

BATAY-CSORBA ARCHITECTS

HIGH PARK RESIDENCE

TORONTO, CANADA

(Above and previous pages) Large windows and skylights above the main entrance, kitchen, and bathroom flood the interior of this home with natural light. (Opposite, top) In contrast to the smooth, brilliant white surfaces of the barrel vault inside the house, the exterior section of the vault is lined with brick. (Opposite, bottom) The rooms on the upper floor of the house are accessed via bridges across the vaulted spaces below.

Cloaked in a Fluid Skin of Bricks Echoing Ancient Tradition

A modern interpretation of historic design, Mohsen Kazemianfard's Saadat Abad Residential Building employs brick to reference the material's use in ancient Iranian architecture. Working with a preexisting seven-story building, the architects developed the facade and updated the interior to enhance the connection between the inside and outside. A glass and concrete tiled exterior is cloaked in a twisted skin of bricks that moves outward to create a space between the layers that the architects call the "expanded border." The fluid brick facade is composed of large, thick bricks, which proved a challenge in the construction, but ultimately paid off with their multifaceted benefits. While providing an aesthetic edge to the facade, the bricks also work to give privacy to residents while still allowing light to enter the building—from the inside, the light playfully scatters across the floor in a checkered pattern. Finally, the brick skin provides thermal protection by absorbing much of the sun's heat in summer and keeps the building warm in winter.

MOHSEN KAZEMIANFARD/ FUNDAMENTAL APPROACH ARCHITECT

SAADAT ABAD RESIDENTIAL BUILDING

TEHRAN, IRAN

(Left and below) Inside the apartments, the walls are lined with brickwork that echoes the perforated design of the facade, albeit in solid form. The effect is to blur the boundaries between inside and outside. (Page 119 and opposite) The building's expanded border allows for rows of planters to line the windows at the front of the building, punctuating the facade with pockets of vegetation.

A Ceramic Latticework Curtain on an Undulating Facade

Despite its skinny stature, Casa Piedrabuena's oscillating frontage makes a distinct mark on the street front. MUKA Arquitectura used bricks of pressed clay to create this ceramic, curtain-like facade, parts of which fold, pivot, and swing open to allow light and air into the home beyond. Steel frames the ceramic material, lending a sturdy resilience to the structure as a whole and complementing the red ceramics with its dark-gray tone. The facade, which is only 8 feet (2.5 meters) wide, transforms throughout the day, with shadow patterns fluctuating as the sun moves across its undulating surface. Behind the ceramic bricks, the home opens up, becoming unexpectedly larger than the front suggests. From inside, the terra-cotta-colored brick latticework of the facade creates everchanging shadows around the interior. The steel beams of the exterior span the ceilings of the interior, which is dominated by a softer and more calming material palette of plywood.

MUKA ARQUITECTURA

CASA PIEDRABUENA

CIUDAD REAL, SPAIN

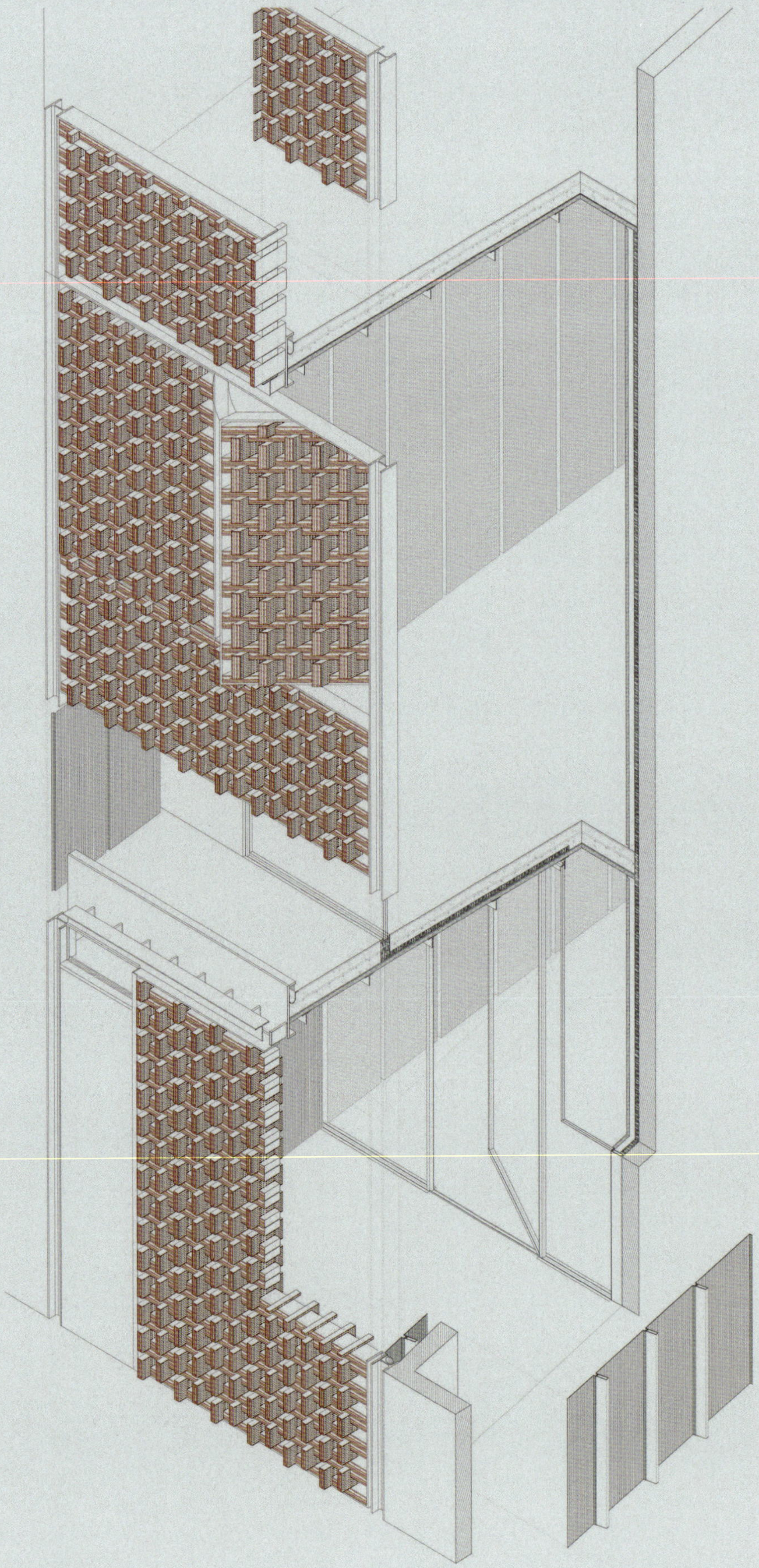

(Opposite and previous pages) Beyond the building's narrow street facade, a flight of stairs takes you to the floor above. Corridors lead to the rear of the house, which widens considerably to create a series of living spaces on each floor. Throughout the building, the walls are lined with OSB boards. (Above) A drawing showing details of the design.

El ajuar

The Ever-Changing Shape, Form, and Function of the Humble Brick

A Brief Look at How Brick-Making Techniques and Architectural Iterations Have Continued to Evolve through Ingenuity and Creativity

Mohsen Kazemianfard architect used preformed brickwork sheets to give this building in Tehran, Iran, a moveable perforated skin.

The term "brick" refers to a building block of hard material, traditionally made from clay and rectangular in shape. Its width, length, and height are such that it can be held in one hand, allowing the other hand free to apply mortar before affixing it to other bricks. Bricks can be used for structural or decorative purposes, and can be classified in many ways—raw material, manufacturing method, or purpose, to name a few. Humans have experimented with materials and methods to craft bricks for thousands of years, so it only makes sense that they continue to evolve along with us.

Mudbricks, also called adobe bricks, are the oldest form of brick. Clay-rich soil is mixed with water, hand formed or pressed into a four-sided wooden mold, removed, and left out to dry under the sun. Clay is formed by mineral deposits that accumulate in the ground, and it is this that enables bricks to be shaped. Tempering the mud with other organic matter—sand, silt, straw, rice husk, banana fibers, animal dung, and/or urine—increases hardness and flexibility, which equals strength. Mudbricks can be laid with wet mud mortar or bitumen and can be plastered with mud, linseed oil, or a mixture using cow manure, for a smooth finish and protection against erosion. While traditional mudbrick construction is still used around the world today, engineers are exploring how to optimize this and other earth-building techniques. For instance, compressed earth bricks (CEB) use a mixture of damp soil, clay, and aggregate, stabilized by Portland cement or lime; a mechanical press is used to form the bricks. For their Intermediate House (2021), in Asunción, Paraguay, Equipo de Arquitectura used compressed earth bricks, stabilized with 10 percent Portland cement, to construct a small home with structural and screen walls as well as a steel-supported vaulted roof.

Fired clay bricks can last hundreds of years without maintenance, and there are now services that source, clean, and sort them, supplying them ready for reuse.

Fired/burnt-clay bricks are what usually come to mind when people hear the word "brick." Exposing clay bricks to extreme heat fuses the clay particles together in a process called vitrification, making them hard and durable. Today, clay and other raw materials are mixed in exact amounts and fired at precise temperatures to create bricks with specific properties, such as hardness, density, surface texture, thermal properties, moisture conductivity, and fire resistance. Bricks fired longer or at a higher temperature are denser and stronger; to make bricks more porous (and better insulating) other organic material, such as sawdust, can be added. During firing, minerals in the clay give color to the bricks as they absorb oxygen. Higher temperatures cause the color to darken: bricks with more iron darken to deep reds or purple/blue; those with less iron and more lime become yellow. Color nuances can be achieved by reducing the amount of oxygen during firing: red turns brownish, while yellow can acquire a green tinge. Their color can be further changed by adding pigments to the clay mix before being fired or by glazing, staining, or painting them afterward.

Clay bricks are shaped in different ways. A common technique is to press them into molds using a hydraulic press. Dry-pressed bricks use a thicker clay mix and are fired for longer. Extruded bricks are forced through a die to create a long cable of the desired width and depth, which is then sliced into bricks by wires. The die can also produce perforated or hollow bricks. The Wall House (2018) by CTA in Bien Hoa, Vietnam, uses multistory walls made of hollow bricks in an unconventional way: while the bricks are normally laid so that the hollows are hidden, in this case, they are turned on their ends to foster air circulation and a sense of permeability between indoors and outdoors.

The clinker brick is one of the many subtypes of fired clay bricks, the name "clinker" coming from the clinking sound the bricks make when struck together. Fired at very high temperatures, they become very hard and darker in color, with a characteristically shiny surface. While their low porosity makes them inferior thermal insulators compared to normal bricks, clinker bricks are highly frost resistant and thus suited for facing and paving. The term can be confusing, as it was historically used both for accidentally over-fired and distorted bricks, as well as for high-quality, intentionally hard bricks—both of which were admired by adherents of the Arts & Crafts Movement in Great Britain and the United States in the late 18th and early 19th centuries, and of brick expressionism in Northern Europe in the early 20th century. Designed by Fritz Höger, the south wing of the Haus Neuerburg cigarette factory (1927) in Hamburg, Germany, is an impressive example of brick expressionism using clinker bricks. Its reinforced concrete structure features a clinker brick facade, embellished with pointed arched windows and columns of twisted clinker brick.

StoneCycling in the Netherlands produces its WasteBasedBricks in a range of colored glazes that include green Cardamom, blue Juniper Berry, and reddy-brown Cloves.

The pattern in which bricks are laid, called the bond, determines both the aesthetics and the stability of a structure. Having staggered rows (called courses) of bricks with offset joints (the mortar bonds) essentially weaves them together. Brick bonding can be quite intricate and require a high degree of craftsmanship. The English bond is the oldest-known and strongest bond and consists of alternating rows of headers—bricks laid with the short side facing out—and stretchers—bricks laid with the long side facing out. Another common bond is the Flemish or Dutch bond, consisting of alternating headers and stretchers in the same course. Hit-and-miss brickwork, sometimes called Brazilian bond, involves skipping or leaving space between the bricks to create a regular pattern of holes, allowing air to circulate and natural light to penetrate the space; in India, this type of perforated wall is known as a brick *jali* (net).

Parametric software now makes it easier for designers to play with variables and achieve complex patterns. The potential of artificial intelligence and bricklaying robots are also being explored. Bricks can be premounted using cladding systems, making installation on-site quicker and easier. For The Interlock (2018), a five-story mixed-use building in London, U.K., Bureau de Change made extensive use of 3D-modeling tools to plan a dynamic brick facade. A total of 5,000 bricks, cast in 44 different sizes from Staffordshire blue clay, appear to twist like cogs. A 1:1 template was used on-site to identify the location of each brick during construction.

Facing bricks and brick veneers, or slips, allow structures to benefit from the aesthetic qualities of brick, even when the underlying structure is different. Facing bricks are full-sized bricks, while brick veneers (slips) are thinner, either slices of standard-size bricks or molded or extruded and wire cut to size. Both types can be premounted using various types of cladding systems for speed, ease of installation, and design flexibility—for instance, for curved facades or indoor walls, or in conjunction with insulated panels. Recent developments also feature cladding systems that can be dismantled easily for recycling.

Alternatives to clay bricks include calcium silicate (sand lime), fly ash (a byproduct of coal-fired power plants), and concrete bricks. Often used for structural masonry, they can be colored for decorative purposes by adding pigments; concrete brick cladding can be made to emulate the look of clay brick, for example. Arguments for their use include the fact that they are less costly to produce and use less energy without the air pollutants associated with firing clay (instead, they harden under pressure). They might also help to eliminate exploitative labor conditions associated with small-scale clay-brick production in some countries.

Recycled brick is gaining appeal as new technologies and infrastructure make it possible to make new building materials from old ones. Bricks made of clay, calcium silicate, and concrete can be crushed and recycled into new bricks or facing tiles, closing the loop in construction.

StoneCycling's WasteBased-Bricks contain at least 60 percent waste rubble from the construction industry and demolition sites.

Close up, the brick-work at Bureau de Change's The Interlock in central London has a cog-like appearance.

For Bureau de Change's The Interlock in central London, computer technology allowed the architects to work beyond the traditional dimension of conventional bricks.

Curved brick features lend a contemporary edge to the facades of a protected historic site in GRAFT architect's sensitive remodeling of post office buildings in Berlin.

Regimented square windows give the revitalized post office facades a sense of geometry amid their curvaceous forms.

At Wall House in Vietnam, all the bricks are reclaimed; burned and blackened bricks introduce variations in color.

The bricks at Wall House are arranged haphazardly, rather than following any traditional bonding method, creating more texture.

A side elevation plan at Wall House, Vietnam. Immediately beyond the entrance to the house is a walled indoor/outdoor courtyard space.

In State of Kin's Brick House in Perth, Australia, traditional stretcher-bond brick walls combine with exposed black steel to conjure an industrial aesthetic.

The clinker brick is one of the many subtypes of fired clay bricks, the name "clinker" coming from the clinking sound the bricks make when struck together. Fired at very high temperatures, they become very hard and darker in color, with a characteristically shiny surface.

StoneCycling produce bricks with a range of different finishes from sand-textured and punch-textured to slice-textured and glazed.

In Mexico City, Iturbide Studio is built with openwork masonry, where double rows of flat, long, stretcher-bond bricks alternate with rows of soldier bricks.

A Symbiotic Addition to a Historic Power Station

Herzog & de Meuron's 10-story addition to the south of Tate Modern's Turbine Hall is a large, folding, and pyramidal brick structure, cut through with horizontal lines of windows. The structure, which is also visible over the top of Tate Modern when approaching the building from the north side, was constructed from the same base palette of bricks as the turbine hall. The brickwork's inclined face is stepped with geometric precision and the brick screen is perforated, allowing light into the museum during both day and night. The combination of texture and perforation allows the brickwork to appear as though it is a veil covering the building's concrete bones. The new Tate Modern structure joins the original building—once a derelict power station—and stands on the site of the power station's switch house. Formerly known as the Bankside 'B' Power Station, it was built in 1947 and decommissioned from use in 1981. The 660-foot- (200-meter-) long building was constructed from a steel frame and clad in some 4.2 million bricks. An impressive 325-foot- (99-meter-) high brick chimney marks the building's midway point. The addition works in symbiosis with the original building, providing a distinct addition to London's skyline without competing with the materiality or structure of the former power station.

HERZOG & DE MEURON

TATE MODERN

2016

LONDON, U.K.

PERFORMING FOR THE CAMERA

Modernist Masterpiece in Pale Brick

A great tower soars above Hilversum Town Hall, signposting the yellow-brick building's location from around the region. Alongside the 157-foot (48-meter) tower, horizontal lines and cubist volumes are hallmarks of this imposing, asymmetrical building. Beneath the tower, a cantilevered canopy dramatically marks the main entrance near the pond. The moderately modernist building's load-bearing structure was developed from steel and concrete, allowing the bricks to defy gravity in some sections and appear to be floating. The pale brick of the building is a particularly noteworthy and contrasting addition to the area, in which many dark-brick homes abound. While the building appears monolithic and militaristic to some, the interior is welcoming and colorful. Dudok purposefully developed an estimated 680,000 unusually elongated bricks for the building. Unfortunately, the majority of the bricks were baked too softly, making them porous and susceptible to frostbite. Consequently, almost all of them were replaced during restoration from 1989 until 1995.

WILLEM MARINUS DUDOK

HILVERSUM TOWN HALL

1931

HILVERSUM, THE NETHERLANDS

Colorful Bricks and Soaring Ceilings

It is the dramatic, lofty, and colorful ceiling of the Hoechst Administration Building main hall that makes the greatest impression on its visitors. Upon entering the building, the dark and low transept that leads to the hall forms a great visual contrast, making the height of the colorful ceiling all the more breathtaking. It is the bricks that add the color to the hall—at the base of the pillars, the bricks are green, and the masonry transitions through a variety of colors as it moves upward. Despite this impressive display, the exterior shouldn't be dismissed. Needing to create a facade from bricks in order to keep the building affordable, Behrens managed to avoid a monotonous and stark exterior by pairing dark and light bricks in patterned contrast. The long building instead becomes an arresting display of three different colors of brick topped with parabola-shaped windows on the upper floor and accompanied by a distinctive tower and bridge over the road. Often associated with brick impressionism, the Hoechst Administration Building was a distinctive and important addition to 20th-century German architecture.

PETER BEHRENS

HOECHST ADMINISTRATION BUILDING

1924

FRANKFURT-HÖCHST, HESSE, GERMANY

OXFAM

An Expansive Brickwork Complex

The revitalization of a historic post office in Berlin's Schöneberg neighborhood saw GRAFT architects develop two new buildings and convert original rooftops into commercial use spaces. All in all, they created a 345,000-square-foot (32,000-square-meter) brick-based complex. The multiple existing post office buildings create several courtyards in which the historic and new brickwork is visible and comparable. Curving brickwork is used around the complex, softening corners and creating irregular wavelike patterns along balconies. The front of one building, which has a sign that (fittingly) reads "BRICKS" has a flowing and stepped brown brickwork pattern that curves inward, cavelike, toward the parabolic entrance door. The textured pattern of this brickwork slowly fades out as it moves up the building, transitioning to flat stretcher-bond brickwork above. Protruding windows across the facade maintain the building's stepped character the entire way up. The project is spectacular in size and while there are variations in dimensions and tone between old and new, the use of brick remains consistent throughout.

GRAFT

BRICKS

BERLIN, GERMANY

(Previous pages) The complex occupies a vast site between two major thoroughfares. Though the elevations are resolutely contemporary, they match their neighbors in height and scale. (Left, below, and opposite) The curving brickwork at both the front and the rear of the building serves to soften the geometry imposed by rows of square windows—some stepping out beyond the brickwork.

OXFAM
denn's

Light Wells Inspired by Bakers' Kilns Jut Out of Agricultural Grounds

Jutting out of a landscape of swaying wheat, Kornets Hus, or House of Grain, makes a dramatic impression on its surroundings. As its name suggests, this cultural information center focuses on the region's rich food and farming culture, and the importance of grain for human civilization. The client, Jørn Ussing Larsen, has been cultivating cereals for almost five decades. He requested that the building houses a 6,5000-square-foot (600-square-meter) visitor center and exhibition space arranged around a bread oven. Reiulf Ramstad Arkitekter drew inspiration from the surrounding landscape—including its wind-polished trees and dark brown soil—and the region's agricultural history. "We were very fascinated by the local architectural vernacular of weather-beaten barns and old farmhouses and could look in any direction to find great sources of inspiration," say the architects. The angular brick volumes create peaks around two brick light wells, which take inspiration from bakers' kilns and become a determining feature at either end of the structure. Inside, large windows frame views of the vast fields of wheat to the west, and light streams into the building down pale Scandinavian-style wood-paneled walls.

REIULF RAMSTAD ARKITEKTER

KORNETS HUS

HJØRRING, NORTH JUTLAND, DENMARK

The single-story, L-shaped information center has an angular light well at each end and flanks two sides of a courtyard garden that looks out across the wheat fields. Inside, a generous, double-height teaching and exhibition space with floor-to-ceiling windows is lined with pale wood. (Opposite) Structurally, the building consists of a timber frame clad in redbrick shingles.

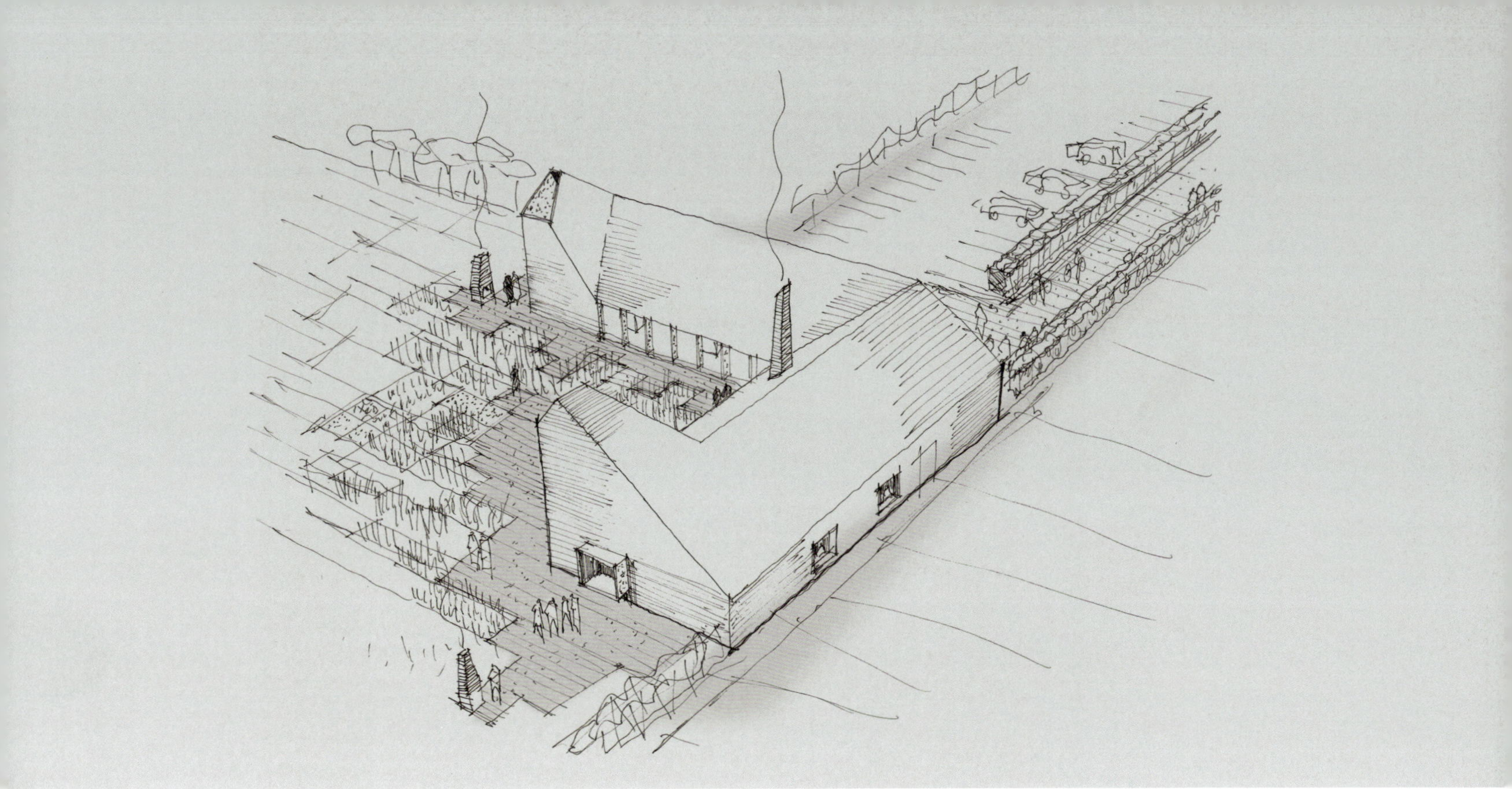

Masonry That Mirrors an Industrial Context

Perimeter House is a two-level residence, with a contrast drawn between the white-brick lower level and a charcoal-gray brick upper. At one end of the site—which is located in an industrial precinct of Abbotsford, Melbourne, and surrounded by brick factories and warehouses—stands the original heritage home. The new perimeter, for which the home is named, is built directly along the boundaries of the property. Studio Bright's use of Architectural Bricks by Adbri Masonry and concrete floors speaks to the historic industrial typology of the area, while a pitched roof and window placements signify the building's residential purpose. "With brick, we were able to generate a gentle curve that captured the living areas throughout the addition, seamlessly connecting interior with exterior," says Studio Bright. These curves are echoed in an outdoor fireplace and the unique white-brick pool, which results in crystal-clear aquamarine water. "The house is a veritable festival of bricks," say the architects, pointing out brick planters, brick-textured surfaces, and walls made from new and recycled bricks. On the rooftop, a perforated brick screen offers partial shade and privacy to the residence, its textural contrast to the solid mass of white bricks below adding a striking visual element.

STUDIO BRIGHT

PERIMETER HOUSE

ABBOTSFORD, MELBOURNE, AUSTRALIA

(Opposite and previous pages) The angular geometry of the facade facing the street contrasts strongly with the soft, curvaceous lines at the rear of the building—a theme that finds echoes in the interior design. The introduction of recessed bricks and perforated sections to the gray-brick facades prevents the upper level of the house appearing too heavy or solid above the white brick walls below.

Modern Exuberance Meets Historic Influence

Occupying the grounds of a decommissioned tile-firing workshop, Brickyard Retreat Renovation pays homage to its historic location in an exuberantly modern manner. Nestled at the foot of the Great Wall in Beigou village, Beijing, Brickyard Retreat is one of the first Chinese rural heritage hotels to be selected as a protected ancient site. Here, carefully considered architectural interventions focus on red bricks and glazed tiles to reflect the heritage of the factory and the history of the village itself. Externally, red brick forms the outline of the curved walls and creates a cohesive traditional style when viewed against the backdrop of the Mutianyu section of Great Wall. The curved brick walls forge serpentine pathways between the buildings, conjuring a sculptural statement when combined with the fluctuating blue, white, and turquoise of the swimming pools. Grass is laid in wavy patterns, and inviting deckchairs border the lawn's edge—each mimicking the shape of the walls and contributing to the joyful nature of the complex. Blue and green are dominant colors; seen in the roof tiling, they present a vivid rendition of the traditional roofs of the area. Internally, the bricks are offset with mosaic floors in natural and bright-orange, blue, and green glazes. These, along with angled ceilings and a series of archways, culminate in a uniquely playful space.

LLLAB.

BRICKYARD RETREAT RENOVATION

BEIGOU VILLAGE, BEIJING, CHINA

(Above and opposite) Exploring the extensive, landscaped grounds of this heritage hotel leads visitors through a series of twisting brick-walled alleyways that open onto small recreation spaces at every turn. Among the features here are a sparkling plunge pool and a raised sundeck overlooking agricultural fields with the Great Wall beyond—a place for quiet and calm contemplation.

(Below) Within the main buildings of the Brickyard hotel complex, a series of terra-cotta brick arches leads from one room to the next, creating long vistas. (Opposite) Brick partitions along the facade create private terraces overlooking the immaculate gardens. Floors are lined with brightly colored, glazed mosaic tiles in blue, green, and orange inside and out.

A Seaside Home Made of Fabric-Like Brickwork

A sprawling project comprised of pale clay brickwork and expansive windows, Bellport House on Long Island, New York, is a calming and distinguished home that does justice to its seaside views and copious light. The home's thin Petersen Tegl bricks are paired with white grout and large windows, giving the home a delicate feel that merges weightlessly with its location, foregrounding its pristine surroundings. The low-set, orthogonal home becomes immersed within the landscape, a feeling that is enhanced by floor-to-ceiling sliding doors that blur the boundaries between inside and out. The random brick bond pattern and slender proportions of the bricks give the walls a fabric-like quality, yet, in contrast, the brickwork provides a robust strength against the corrosive salty ocean air and damp winters of the region. The thermal mass of the material also ensures ease of heating and cooling year-round. Continuing the subtle and calming aesthetic of the brickwork is a natural interior palette of travertine floors, soft walls made from sawn wood panels, and white ceilings.

TOSHIHIRO OKI

BELLPORT HOUSE

BELLPORT,
LONG ISLAND,
NEW YORK, USA

Pale clay bricks, whitewashed walls, and generous glazing combine to create spaces of pure light and brightness set against the green of their verdant surroundings. There is wonderful variance in the colors of the Petersen Tegl bricks—from chalk white and cream to biscuit and even cinnamon tones. Collectively, they give the walls a patina more readily associated with reclaimed brick.

Bricks of Optical Illusion in an Infinite Loop

On one side of the outside space in the aptly named Twisting Courtyard, brick paving morphs and curves into a wall, a feature that continues through a glass window and into the home. This mirage-like focal point brings an eccentric and unexpected energy to the *siheyuan*, an archetypal historic Chinese residence composed of a courtyard surrounded by buildings on each side. "The design aims at getting rid of the solemn and stereotyped impression given by *siheyuan*, and creating an open and active living atmosphere," says ARCHSTUDIO. The modern curves of the brick courtyard contrast with the buildings' historic roofs and the white stones that fill the recesses. By continuing from the outdoors to the interior, the gray curved and twisting brickwork creates a symbiosis and cohesion between the areas. Inside, the curved wall takes shape as a brick curtain that hides auxiliary areas such as the kitchen, restroom, and storage. The curving bricks also feature in the bathroom ceiling, where they bring a moment of optical intrigue in an otherwise almost clinical space. Meanwhile, the public areas for socializing, such as the dining room—in which an expansive glass pane makes up one wall—are visible to the courtyard. The juxtaposition of new and old continues inside the house, where pristine white walls create a gallery-like space below antique rafters that hint at the narrative history of the location.

ARCHSTUDIO

TWISTING COURTYARD

PAIZIHUTONG, BEIJING, CHINA

The black bricks snake through the house and its central courtyard, creating an infinite loop that gives the design a tremendous sense of fluidity and motion. There is an air of surrealism as the loop breaks the boundaries between inside and outside, often reflected in the windows so that its visual impact is mirrored in places. The use of a limited palette throughout only emphasizes the effect.

Circular Motifs Contrast Tessellating Patterns

Designed to make the delineation between outside and inside ambiguous, Casa UC, on the outskirts of Morelia, Mexico, is a house of deep contemplation. Brick was chosen for its timeless qualities and as a reminder "of what our soil and grounds provide us," says architect Daniela Bucio Sistos. A large focus of the residence was to build mindfully, using local materials and artisans. Made up of slim, artisanal bricks from Ciudad Hidalgo, the brickwork features regular indentations, creating a textured effect. Light flows into the hallway through a slatted roof, to cast additional patterns on the already tessellated walls—a simple but dynamic visual effect. "The main challenge of using the brick was to hide every column or inner structure so that the brick walls were as clean visually as possible," says Sistos. Inside, concrete flooring, wood paneling, and bespoke timber cabinetry all create strong, hard lines. The square structure and rich brickwork are softened here and there via a repeated circular motif in feature windows, door handles, ceiling lighting, and a spectacular overhead form in the main courtyard.

DANIELA BUCIO SISTOS

CASA UC

MORELIA, MICHOACÁN, MEXICO

There is great harmony in the geometry of the design, where the rectilinear forms of the building are offset by round windows and curvaceous forms in the grounds. The concrete flooring, wood paneling, and bespoke timber cabinetry all contribute to the warm, earthy tones that characterize the building, helping it to blend in beautifully with its immediate surroundings.

The house is surrounded by verdant outdoor spaces, rich with vegetation, and a generous, partially covered central courtyard occupies space at the heart of the design. There is a constant play of light and shade on the interior and exterior surfaces as the sun moves across the sky, streaming through slatted roofs and catching the texture of the brickwork walls.

Minimalist Lines Broken by a Circular Motif

A large, glazed, concrete circle is set within the brickwork facade of this modernist-style Indian home, just one element of the project's minimalist yet striking geometry. Exposed concrete overhangs the facade, which features additional windows. The clients requested a "vastu" compliant house—the term referring to a traditional Indian system of architecture that determines the design principles, layout, and measurements of the home. As such, the 7,395-square-foot (687-square-meter) home revolves around a series of connections that emphasize the relationship between indoor and outdoor as well as the interrelation between the different rooms and levels. Doors between the living spaces fold and slide open, allowing for the creation of individual rooms, or large, open and connected spaces. The minimalist palette continues internally, prioritizing bricks, concrete, and wood. In the bedrooms, redbrick feature walls contrast with dark-gray polished cement floors. Breaking up any monotony, the circular motif seen on the facade repeats throughout the home, delivering an unexpected counter to the strong linear form of the building. On a balcony upstairs, for example, a circle of bricks frames a window in a cement wall, through which a view of the surrounding greenery enters.

TRAANSPACE

THE BRICK CONNECTION

VADODARA, INDIA

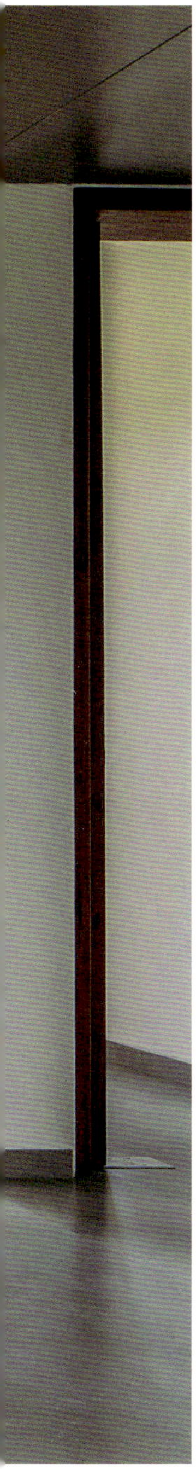

(Previous pages and opposite) Symmetry is a significant feature here, in the structural elements mirrored on the building's facade, in the alignment of internal doorways, and in the arrangement of furniture. (Above) Interior spaces are carefully curated and include a minimal selection of primarily wood furnishings within a very limited palette of warm grays, taupes, and browns.

Clean lines are a hallmark of this house. Aside from the intermittent circular features—at the entrance, on the roof, and within custom-made shelving, the rooms, furnishings, and structural elements are fiercely rectilinear, an aspect that is accentuated by the stretcher-bond brick-work that dominates the design both inside and out.

A Home More Intricate than Its Name Suggests

An array of contrasting brickwork shapes combines to form a striking and eye-catching facade in the aptly named Brick House. Architects State of Kin have used the material to conceive a dwelling that is not quite as simple as it suggests. The sweeping two-level home pays homage to the area's industrial past, using an uncomplicated material palette of reclaimed brick, concrete, steel, and glass. On the front facade, black-steel frames the windows and makes up the garage doors and fencing. The bricks, as well as the steel, continue inside the building, making for richly textured spaces. Playful elements, such a second-floor reading net that looks over the first-floor living area, and a bright pop of yellow paint on the elevator doors, extend the quirkiness inherent in the facade. Bricks are used exploratively throughout; a basement room sees polished concrete floors paired with a herringbone-patterned brickwork ceiling, and beside the elevator and around the home, checkerboard patterns feature voids in the brickwork to allow light and air to move through the home.

STATE OF KIN

BRICK HOUSE

PERTH,
AUSTRALIA

(Opposite and following pages) The black-steel structural elements contrast perfectly with the exposed brickwork to give the home a light-industrial edge. The concept is taken one step further in the quirky, factory-type elevation the architects have given the building (previous pages) which feels all the more authentic, thanks to the rich patination of the reclaimed bricks.

The Versatile, Adaptable, and Sustainable Nature of Bricks

Our Unavoidable Climate Emergency, and the Need for Urban and Rural Rehabilitation, Pressingly Calls for the Use of Brick to Aid in Low-Cost and Low-Maintenance Construction

Fuyang Cultural Complex near Hangzhou, China, epitomizes Amateur Architecture Studio's passion for cladding building in reclaimed materials.

Brick pays homage to the context, the site, the people, and the history that surrounds it. Baked clay is one of the most compliant construction materials, its versatility allowing for adaptation in a range of climates. Traditions for making bricks by hand vary from place to place but, ideally, true clay is rid of sediment or stone before being mixed into mud—sometimes with added grass or sand—and poured into molds to let dry before "cooking" in a kiln (firing).

Traditional fired brick is an exceptional material for regulating extreme temperatures. In the border city of Matamoros, at the very edge of northeast Mexico, Colectivo C733's open-air market sits below huge inverted-brick trapezoid shapes surrounding a central courtyard that is open to the sky. The design allows heat to rise and escape while at the same time letting in sunlight and ventilation.

In rural Rwanda, the most densely populated country in Africa, the need for adequate housing calls for straightforward single-family-oriented and affordable solutions. A team of MIT Africa students led by Professor Rafi Segal designed a Prototype Village House in 2018, which purposefully was not clad in the traditional sun-dried bricks but rather in red fired bricks that would last much longer. Core panels made of compressed straw fiber with concrete posts reinforce the brick walls.

Historically, bricks were always made locally. One of the simplest methods involved tightly packing earth and pressing it by hand. This process has withstood time and continues today, boosted by the introduction of compression machines. Operated or powered by hand, such machines have led to the creation of a more efficient and sustainable material. Compressed earth bricks (CEB), for example, made using laterite soil that is similar to, yet lower maintenance than, adobe. CEB are still made using local materials, sometimes on-site. They face some upkeep issues, however, as bricks exposed to the elements—particularly moisture—deteriorate if not constructed properly.

Historically, bricks were always made locally. One of the simplest methods involved tightly packing earth and pressing it by hand. This process has withstood time and continues today.

Oftentimes industrially made bricks find their quality is not up to par—imperfections in color, size, and finish are not uncommon. Such bricks are set aside and almost always end up as waste. Luckily, many architects resort to collecting materials like these and repurposing them.

Chinese architects Wang Shu and Lu Wenyu of Amateur Architecture have found there is a ready supply of such materials and that their makers are frequently more than willing to give surplus bricks away for free. One of the most innovative ways this duo has found for repurposing rejected and recycled bricks is in their application of *wa pan,* a Chinese building technique that features a patchwork of recycled clay matter and that is traditionally used to repair damage caused by typhoons. This method is most visible in their Fuyang Cultural Complex, where the architectural design is highlighted and its character brought to life through an array of recycled bricks and tiles arranged in a seemingly arbitrary fashion. The success of this, and other buildings designed by Amateur Architecture, is proof that quality construction need not rely on big budgets or necessitate shiny, new bricks.

Another visionary example is that of the Muuratsalo Experimental House in Jyväskylä, Finland, designed by Alvar Aalto and his second wife Elissa in the 1950s, using leftover bricks from Aalto's Säynätsalo Town Hall. Their summer home is a patchwork of clay bricks and ceramic tiles that wrap around a central courtyard. Aalto's work is known for avoiding modern artificial materials in visible places and for creating spaces that have a direct connection to nature where, as architect and writer Michael Trencher notes, "components are overlaid one on top of another—rocks, stones, trees, and water—they all interact in a dynamic manner. Every space in nature is unique, there is no repetition of that space." Trencher continues by stating that Aalto "recognized and understood the dynamic elements in human activities, and, therefore, we as human beings are naturally attuned to our operating of that kind of space."

A WasteBasedBrick from StoneCycling in the Netherlands, a firm dedicated to making new bricks from old construction materials.

Last but not least, is the legacy of India-based architect Laurie Baker, whose design-build method avoided the traditional contractor and other intermediaries and left the work, as architect Himanshu Burte wrote for *The Architectural Review,* in the trusted hands of its main characters: architect, client, and craftsman, while taking the opportunity to use discarded materials for a low cost. Baker, like Aalto, opted for unplastered and unwhitewashed red brick and experimented widely with latticed walls with *jali* openings, and, more importantly, never stopped learning from local masons.

In Chiapas, Mexico, a group of students from the Universidad Autónoma de Chiapas and the University of São Paulo, Brazil, developed a prefabricated system as an alternative to the popular joist-and-vault roofing system called Domotej. For La Casa del Abuelo—a project that aims to benefit vulnerable or neglected seniors—a series of concave 38.5 × 38.5-inch (98 × 98-centimeter) units were laid out with annealed red bricks arranged *petatillo*-style (cross-hatched) on the ground, joined with mortar, and reinforced with wire. Each unit was then easily aligned in a series of C-section beams before a layer of concrete was cast with a reinforcement mesh on top. The result represents a move toward the possibility of adaptable and self-constructed social housing.

The inevitability of the climate emergency calls for timely solutions, one of which is to rebuild places for shelter following a natural disaster. Grassroots organizations such as Re_Construir Mexico joined the collaborative effort to rebuild 50 homes throughout the country after the devastating September 2017 earthquake. One such home, Casa Martha in Mexico (named for the home's matriarch), was designed by Naso architects and is a functional example that not only provides adequate, low-cost housing, but also improves the quality of life of families living in poverty.

Perilous living conditions are a characteristic of much informal construction on the outskirts of Mexico City. Palmas House, designed by Dosa Studio, provided a strategically planned solution for a family that had previously inhabited a precarious building on the site for more than 40 years. The modular brick home now includes an open courtyard and its sawtooth roof is oriented so that sunlight regulates temperature throughout the house.

In Quang Ninh province, Vietnam, H&P Architects are rethinking the human relationship to nature and agriculture in an increasingly polluted and overpopulated zone. AgriNesture is a prototype for clusterlike housing that might be suitable for sites prone to flooding and could help revitalize agriculture in low-income areas. Here, rammed earth and bricks make up the walls and partitions and a green roof designed for agriculture features an integrated rainwater-harvesting system.

Experimentation has led StoneCycling to use all manner of waste materials to produce its WasteBasedBricks.

As for durability, Indian-based studio PMA madhushala took from the vernacular *gadi* house typology to build a sustainable environment around a central skylight with "passive" climate- and energy-controlling systems, along with self-sustained gardens that allow for independent living conditions. The load-bearing base wall is made of stone and brick and is strong enough to withstand earthquakes and to hold its feature wavelike, breezy brick wall above.

StoneCycling combine the latest technologies with age-old hand-crafting traditions to create its WasteBasedBricks.

Rather than demolish decaying walls at The Parchment Works in the U.K., Will Gamble Architects incorporated them into its design.

At Matamoros market in Mexico, the brick exterior of the innovative roof structure helps provide insulation.

Galvanized sheet metal lines the huge, trapezoid roof structures of Matamoros market, reflecting the fierce midday heat away from the space below.

The design of the vaulted brick roof at Crossway, Kent, helps the building to retain heat.

Crossway in Kent, England, features a large, vaulted brick roof made using locally sourced materials and covered in earth.

At StoneCycling in the Netherlands, many of the brick-making processes are carried out by hand.

The patchwork facade of Amateur Architecture Studio's Fuyang Cultural Complex near Hangzhou in China.

Oftentimes industrially made bricks find their quality is not up to par—imperfections in color, size, and finish are not uncommon. Such bricks are set aside and almost always end up as waste. Luckily, many architects resort to collecting materials like these and repurposing them.

Raw materials at the StoneCycling plant in the Netherlands.

Casa Martha in Mexico is built using adoblocks that were created onsite for a sustainable design that can be easily replicated across the region.

The Hat Factory That Wears Its Own Pointy Hat

The site of a former hat factory, the dye-works section of Hutfabrik Friedrich Steinberg, Herrmann & Co. itself appears to be wearing a hat—a charcoal-toned geometric protrusion rising above its pale-brick base, resembling the cross section of a fedora. Designed by renowned German expressionist architect and pioneer of art deco and streamline moderne architecture, Erich Mendelsohn, the factory was built in a modern industrial architectural style. Sitting on an elongated site, the factory takes shape as a series of buildings that includes the dyeworks, four production halls, and a power center. It is constructed from reinforced concrete girders and exterior brick-curtain walls beneath a roof coated in a rubber surface. The bricks on the exterior walls are placed in horizontal layers, with each alternate layer protruding from, or receding into, the surface. At each end of the warehouse buildings, a triangular pattern is cut into the brickwork to make way for angled windows. These brick patterns, added simply for their aesthetic nature, are examples of brick expressionism.

ERICH MENDELSOHN

HUTFABRIK
FRIEDRICH STEINBERG,
HERRMANN & CO.

1923

LUCKENWALDE,
BRANDENBURG,
GERMANY

A Diamond Nestled in Nature

A wall of brickwork diamonds hangs, curtain-like, along the rear facade of House DG. Held up by a black-steel beam, the unique design is composed of long, thin, dark-brown bricks and acts as a sun shield for the living areas and bedrooms at the back of the house. The same bricks continue in a more repetitive and standard stretcher-bond pattern around the rest of the facade, creating a strong and impressive structure. Built sustainably, this home nestles within nature, with native trees surrounding it and a stream flowing at the rear of the property. Breaking up the dark facade, a clear blue pool and light-cement terrace sit beneath the diamond brickwork curtain. Large glass sliding doors lead into the kitchen and living area, where the bricks cease and a variety of natural materiality and tones begins; textured creamy walls are paired with timber kitchen cabinets, a fireplace suspended over a cowhide rug brings warmth to a living area, and blackened-wood walls join copper fittings in the bathroom.

LENS°ASS ARCHITECTEN

HOUSE DG

KAMPENHOUT, FLEMISH BRABANT, BELGIUM

(Previous pages and opposite) The building's dark brickwork complements the natural landscape, its earthy tones echoing those of the surrounding trees. (Above) The diamond brickwork wall creates an intriguing inside/outside space between the pool and the home's true interior; beside the swimming pool, an external flight of stairs leads up to rooms on the second floor.

Thanks to the honeycomb design of the curtain-like brickwork facade, the home's interiors are filled with diffuse light. A wood-burning stove takes center stage in the open-plan living room space and furnishings are kept to a minimum throughout. Among the more quirky features are lights suspended at a rakish angle to hang above the dining-room table halfway across the room.

Brickwork Nestled Within a Former Warehouse

A perforated-redbrick structure rises up between the walls of a former warehouse in this Lisbon waterfront home. Located in an area of manufacturing and logistic warehouses, Casa Altinho takes cues from its industrial surroundings and the original building itself to merge house with warehouse in paying homage to the historic warehouses in the district. Externally, the volume of brick on the three-story home reflects the shape and scale of the original building, with its pitched roof and sharp corners. The density of the brickwork ebbs and flows, allowing light to enter the home selectively through a latticed pattern across the facade in some parts and closing off the facade entirely where privacy is needed. *Altinho* refers to the dwelling's elevated position in the city, and one end of the home looks out toward the river. Internally, in the lower part of the house, a run of brickwork barrel vaults supported by steel beams complements the historic textured walls and cobblestone floors. It is the steel beams that provide the framework of the home, allowing the two volumes to coexist. More contemporary rendered walls and large windows accompany the brickwork upstairs.

ANTÓNIO COSTA LIMA ARQUITECTOS

CASA ALTINHO

LISBON, PORTUGAL

On the second floor of the house, a large open-plan room has two fully glazed gable ends. At the end that houses the kitchen (opposite), the glazing overlooks an atrium and, beyond that, a perforated brick wall. At the opposite end—the one that faces the sea—the glazing is open to the view, encased within the steel frame (pages 208–209), which also houses a generous balcony.

(Left, below, and previous page) Set on three floors, the interior of Casa Altinho reveals a complex arrangement of spaces that include split-level rooms, internal courtyards, hammock floors, and glazed voids. The central wooden staircase appears to float as it climbs from one floor to the next. Bricks feature inside the house as well as outside, in the barrel-vaulted ceilings in the bedrooms.

Inside Out: The Use of Brickwork in Interior Design

Open Courtyards and Lattice Walls Shifting Light and Shadow Make Way for the Uninterrupted Introduction of Natural Brick in the Home

Whitewashed walls combine with black-steel window frames to conjure a minimalist vibe at Beatty Vermeiren's Pattern House in Cape Town, South Africa.

Brickwork in interior architecture is arguably one of the most flexible choices since it can either expand rooms in any direction to create earthy, elegant, or breezy spaces, or it can provide nesting places of solace and meditation. Yet, one of the most advantageous characteristics of brickwork is that it is not necessary to define where the exterior ends and the interior begins. Bricks offer an opportunity to continue rooms, stairs, and ceilings from the outside well into the interior.

Vaulted ceilings, for example, are a common feature of interior brickwork because of their ability to create large open-plan spaces. Near the city of Puerto Escondido, on Mexico's South Pacific Coast, Casa Volta by the architects Ambrosi Etchegaray is an example of an unassuming, open-plan design made by efficiently repurposing material to create three barrel-vaulted structures. Covering roughly 1,290 square feet (120 square meters), the kitchen, dining area, and bedrooms are placed along rectangular plans interconnected by reflecting still-water pools that render the volumes weightless. The rooms are enveloped in terra-cotta material that keeps them shaded and ventilated. Wood-framed reed screens are used as sliding doors and at the end of each vault for air circulation.

Structural brickwork can likewise complement interior design. In Mexico City, a work studio for photographer Graciela Iturbide, designed by Mauricio Rocha + Gabriela Carrillo architects, is one with stellar use of purposely unembellished brickwork throughout the entire building. Thick wood frames floor-to-ceiling windows that overlook an enclosed, triple-height patio surrounded by brick latticework. Long wooden beams reminiscent of hacienda architecture capture the rural feel of the design in the interior and pair well with the distinct patterns on floors, walls, and screens.

Experimenting with changes in patterns and arrangement using fired red bricks along with other natural materials can provide pleasing aesthetic results, especially out in nature.

Cinder-block walls can be traced to other traditions in the use of screens—the mashrabiya windows of Islamic architecture or Japanese privacy lattice screens among them. In places where privacy and safety are primary concerns, houses tend to look in rather than out with the use of blind walls complemented by open courtyards.

The use of brick in interiors can render the need for any further materials or finishes obsolete. Retail architecture presents good examples of this and provides a great resource for potentially adapting elements in residential interiors. Architect Frida Escobedo's design for the Aesop Store in Park Slope, Brooklyn, is built of handmade compacted earth tiles made in the Mixteca Region of Oaxaca, Mexico. While not necessarily efficient—the bricks took more than eight weeks to make—their beautiful natural pink pigment makes these custom-designed pieces a unique decorative asset.

Like cinder-block screens and latticework, glass bricks have the quality of letting light shine outward at night, like lanterns. Taking cues from La Maison de Verre designed by Pierre Chareau in Paris in 1932, glass-brick walls have had many comebacks since, and contemporary practice is not the exception. Depending on the thickness and transparency of the glass brick, privacy can even be of little concern. The Glassbook House, described by its creators at Sibling Architects as "a light-filled sanctuary for reading," is a traditional brick home on the front that is then clad in glass blocks around the sides and toward the back, for a fully covered glass-brick wall. A contemporary take on Chareau's design, the interior incorporates a metal staircase, mesh floors, and a plywood two-story bookcase. What's more, the bricks help muffle the sound of the nearby airport.

In Paizihutong, Dashilar Area, Beijing, a former *siheyuan* historic house with a central garden has been refurbished by ARCHSTUDIO and renamed Twisting Courtyard. A continuous carpet of dark-gray bricks swirls through the floors, walls, and ceilings unifying the entire space inside and out.

Mixing glazed and raw clay bricks can render surprisingly complementary textures and provide fluctuation and easy transitions within interior spaces. The Daylesford Longhouse by Partners Hill in Australia, home to a boutique farm, garden kitchen, cooking school, reception venue, and the owners' home, is a new take on the rural farmhouse. Glazed white bricks laid with orange grout, however, make the sky-lit bathroom one of the most exciting rooms in the 328-foot- (110-meter-) long "shed."

Glazed walls at Mexico City's Iturbide Studio avoid interrupting the rhythm of the brickwork as it transitions from inside to outside.

Many houses made of brick feature smooth, plastered finishes on the interiors. However, there are other ways to incorporate bricks inside the home, such as the enclosed, windowed terraces with open garden views toward textured brick walls seen at the Casuarina House designed by Vokes and Peters in Brisbane.

Experimenting with changes in patterns and arrangement using fired red bricks along with other natural materials can provide pleasing aesthetic results, especially out in nature. In the mountains of Jumilla, Spain, a place for refuge named La Casa del Ángel stands along a hiking path. The existing structure was clad in a variety of Aspe ceramic tiles and clay bricks, including perforated blocks above the windows to allow permanently for ventilation and shade. Both the interior and the exterior, with a built-in bench, invite passersby to take rest and connect with the landscape.

The design of the 1997 Casa Riofrio in Cundinamarca, Colombia, creates a microcosm of geometry, texture, shelter, and spectacle, and is an example that brings the possibilities of exposed brick into the interior of the home. Jaime and Isabelle's award-winning home in Palma, Mallorca by TEd'A arquitectes is another fine example of this.

Interconnected courtyards feature in the work of Bijoy Jain of Studio Mumbai. The architect honors the nature and anonymity of the clay material and our connection to it with the craftsmanship of the Ahmedabad House built using handmade local brick. The house's geometric planes are designed to interact with the nature of changing shadows, the reflections from the dark-green pool in the courtyard, and the shifts in temperature throughout the day.

Patchwork that involves the use of different materials, or even just variations on textures and forms of brick, allows for decorative and structural applications. It also allows an architect to pay homage to the site and the context of the building. The design of the Gallery House by Abin Design Studio, a multipurpose community space in Bansberia, West Bengal, is inspired by local temples and was made using leftover industrial ceramic blocks and local terra-cotta bricks and was built working together with local artisans.

Brick can also come in polychromatic shades and finishes according to the clay used, the firing temperature, or the use of glazing. The brick manufacturer Petersen Tegl in Denmark is known for crafting multihued bricks with different finishes for varying purposes. In the clay shingle facade of Tikari Works' apartment building, The Rye, these bricks lend a sculptural quality to the building. Petersen Tegl's Kolumba brick collection, developed in 2000 with Swiss architect Peter Zumthor for the Kolumba Museum in Cologne, Germany, has since been applied in places like the Henne Kirkeby Kro, Denmark by Tegnestuen Mejeriet. Here the bricks were used for the interior and exterior and paired with the site's original 1790 West Jutland local bricks made from mud stomped on by livestock before firing. Also in Denmark, Fjordenhus in Vejle, the first building by artist Olafur Eliasson and the architectural team at his studio, recalls Louis Kahn's National Assembly Building in Dhaka, Bangladesh, but with a distinct characteristic—namely, its 15 different tones of unglazed brick, each perfectly fit within the complex curved forms and arched windows.

At ARCHSTUDIO's Twisting Courtyard in Beijing, China, black bricks take shape as a path, as a wall, and as a ceiling as they loop their way around the development.

Bright-red stack-bonded bricks with white grout create a lively grid at Hive House, London, designed by Nimtim Architects.

Exposed brickwork can become pivotal in creating a look. At Brick House in Perth, Australia, the aim was to reflect the industrial heritage of the home's location.

Heavily textured brick walls are a hallmark of the interior spaces at Wallmakers' Pirouette House in Kerala, India.

At Iturbide Studio, long wooden beams mirror the linear patterns of the brickwork, serving to make the rooms look and feel longer.

At Casa Martha in Mexico, exposed adob-locks contribute to the rustic charm of the interior spaces.

Clean lines and symmet-rical arrangements reinforce the modernist principles that informed TRAANSPACE's design for The Brick Connection in Vadodara, India.

A Catalan vault creates dynamic spaces at Sameep Padora & Associates' Maya Somaiya Library in Kopargaon, India.

In the kitchen at Pirouette House, Kerala, the exposed brick ends are encased in cement to create a smooth-walled surface below the cupboards.

The use of brick in interiors can render the need for any further materials or finishes obsolete. Retail architecture presents good examples of this and provides a great resource for potentially adapting elements in residential interiors.

Kennedy Nolan's Caroline House in Melbourne, Australia, has a concave exterior that creates beautifully curved walls in interior spaces.

At Pirouette House, Kerala, the hard-edged, exposed brick, cement, and steel surfaces are softened by the addition of locally sourced cane.

Bricks for Passive Thermal Regulation

Just southwest of Barcelona, near the center of Castelldefels, the Casa 1311 site is surrounded by neighboring homes with bougainvillea, climbing plants, and lush vegetation. Hoping to stimulate the greenery to extend onto this plot, HARQUITECTES designed a purpose-built residence to encourage growth, and made a predominant Peruvian pepper plant a focal point of the landscaping. The house itself is defined by the architects' choice of brick—an atypical 12-inch (30-centimeter) ceramic block by Wienerberger, favored for its passive thermal regulation properties. The cubed forms fluctuate from pale terra-cotta to warm ocher in color, giving the building's facade its characteristic brindled appearance—an effect that is enhanced by the unique ridged surfaces of the bricks. At the entrance of the house, a rectangle of bricks is arranged to serve as a doormat. The surrounding trees provide protection from solar radiation during the hottest months, while the inclination of the roof with large windows allows for natural sunlight in winter and cross ventilation in summer. Inside, a more traditional brick lines the floor, introducing a charmingly rustic and warm atmosphere.

HARQUITECTES

CASA 1311

CASTELLDEFELS, BARCELONA, SPAIN

A single-story house, Casa 1311 has two sloping roofs below which a run of windows brings natural light into the rooms of the house, compensating for the shade cast by the surrounding trees. Inside, finishes are quite basic, with surface-mounted electricity conduits, hardwood door and window frames, stainless-steel kitchen elements, and raw or polished concrete ceilings and floors.

Material for Form and Functionality

Casa Martha's distinctive, curved white rooftop rises above dense greenery in an area that sits between the renowned archaeological site of Malinalco and the pilgrim town of Chalma. The rooftop is a distinguishing characteristic of this otherwise low-set, unostentatious home. The two stories of light-gray adoblock earth bricks are interspersed with symmetrically placed ocher-framed windows, a color that also accents the exterior staircase handrail and the sliding red doors of the lower floor. The home was conceived under exceptional circumstances in which Naso was invited to participate in a project to reconstruct one of 50 houses that were damaged during an earthquake that struck the area in 2017. The home is designed to host a multigenerational family and ensure accessibility for the aging parents. The adoblocks were created on-site, allowing the material to be moved with easy efficiency. "Within our architectural design it was interesting how all the spatial qualities and proportions were dictated by the block dimensions and physical aspect, which made the house unique in terms of aesthetics and functionality," says the architect.

NASO

CASA MARTHA

MALINALCO, MEXICO

(Page 224, left, and below) An external staircase leads to a bedroom beneath the building's domed roof and a terrace with views across the open countryside. (Page 225 and opposite) On the first floor, the primary rooms of the family home are accessed through glazed sliding doors. The red ocher of the doors and windows finds echoes in the dry earth surrounding the house.

A compact first floor comprises two bedrooms, a bathroom, and an open-plan kitchen/dining area. The roof overhangs to provide a shaded outside space. Rudimentary kitchen appliances are cast in a concrete unit and the furniture and kitchen cabinetry are made from wood to utilitarian designs. Bare-brick walls contribute to the rustic interior.

Stack-Bonded Brickwork Creates a Lively Grid

Based on a brief that requested an expanded family living space including the kitchen, dining room, additional study spaces, and a room for entertaining, Hive House was born. The extension to this Edwardian terraced house in South London is subtle and unpretentious yet brings character through its contrasting materiality and palette. "It was driven by principles of simplicity and honesty, and influenced by a modest budget but also a shared vision to create something unpretentious but materially and spatially rich," say nimtim architects. Inside, the walls are uniquely crafted with a stack-bonded brick pattern made from 2.5-inch (6.4-centimeter) Farnham Red facing bricks and recessed white mortar. This contrast creates a gridded pattern, the geometry of which finds echoes in the pale timber shelving, ceiling, and the gridded baby-pink and sage tiles, all of which add to the lightweight liveliness of the extension. The brickwork doesn't function as a structural necessity to the home; rather, it adds cladding and robustness, as well as a reference to the original exposed brick at the entrance of the house. The brickwork continues externally onto the terrace as paving.

NIMTIM ARCHITECTS

HIVE HOUSE

LONDON, U.K.

This extension cleverly combines a structural plywood frame with stack-bonded brickwork cladding internally and externally. Inside the house, the plywood is exposed in places to provide useful storage. On the outside, besides the brickwork, a patinated lead fascia protects the plywood from the elements, contrasting beautifully with dark-gray aluminum door frames.

A Monolith of Privacy and Peace

One side of this Mexican home by Esrawe Studio presents a monolithic, windowless wall made of dark, red-brown bricks—a somewhat stern and imposing structure. Yet around the corner, a sunken courtyard with verdant, jungle-like landscaping offsets this initial impression of Casa Sierra Fría. The U-shaped building houses four bedrooms—built to host a family—a luxurious wine cellar, and a rooftop terrace (evidence of the family's plans for entertaining, despite the almost hostile exterior of their home).

The entrance to the house is also striking, with an oversized-wooden door that swings wide open to an interior that is lighter than expected, given the external brickwork. Here is an illuminated yet introspective and private retreat. A combination of pale stone, wood, and white walls, along with more plants, contributes to a chic and modern atmosphere. The contrast between the strong brick exterior and the softer, lighter interiors allows what is an impressive and seemingly impermeable home on the outside to feel sheltered, familiar, and private on the inside.

ESRAWE STUDIO

CASA SIERRA FRÍA

MEXICO CITY, MEXICO

(Previous pages and above) As you approach the house, you see there are no windows on the deep-red brick facade, but a large wooden door interrupts the brickwork and swivels open to reveal an interior with almost fully glazed walls. Stairs leading to the first floor of the house have a few stone treads at the bottom, transitioning to wooden treads cantilevered from the wall.

(Opposite, top) The long, slender bricks make up the exterior walls and floors of this elegant home, and line the spaces that surround the building. (Opposite, bottom; and below) Inside the house, raw-concrete walls, floors, and ceilings find echoes in the paved stone floor of the sunken courtyard at the heart of the dwelling. (Bottom) The bathroom is lined with gray marble.

Once Modernist Homes, Now Contemporary Art Museums

Flat roofs and dark-brick cuboid structures are two of the external determining characteristics of Haus Esters and Haus Lange. Built for German industrialists Hermann Lange and Josef Esters, the structures are two neighboring Bauhaus homes. Considered a pioneer of modernist architecture, German-American architect Ludwig Mies van der Rohe designed the buildings to connect with the natural views. From the street side, the homes appear as rigid, flat surfaces, but on the side facing the parklike gardens, steps trickle down into nature and large windows overlook the greenery. The main structure of each home was designed as a series of interlocking steel cubes, with the brick stucco exterior having an aesthetic function rather than being used for its load-bearing properties. This structural decision meant that large windows could be cut into the facade, something that would not have been possible with brick walls. In recent years, the two buildings have become immortalized in their role as the Kunstmuseen Krefeld, a contemporary art museum.

LUDWIG MIES
VAN DER ROHE

HAUS ESTERS
AND HAUS LANGE

1930

KREFELD,
GERMANY

A White, Windswept Home on South Africa's Southern Cape

Emerging from the greenery on the coastal slopes of Chapmans Peak, Cape Town, the white-painted bricks and black-framed windows of Pattern House offer a minimalist contrast to the building's windswept and rugged surroundings. The client's brief was simple: to design a three-bedroom home that maximized both light and views. Referencing the vernacular architecture of the cape, clay bricks were used in the construction—on the one hand, to blend in with the local historic aesthetic, but also to achieve a handmade architectural style using elemental materials. In order to achieve this handmade feel, the architects used bricks from a local brickyard, which have a crafted, imperfect, and textured character, in preference to more uniform mass-produced alternatives. Older homes in the area were traditionally painted with white limewash, and similarly, Pattern House's bricks were painted to allow the play of light and shadow on its surface. Bricks form the structural core of the home, without concrete or steel reinforcement, while cement is used as the interior flooring and steel acts as frames for the doors and windows.

BEATTY VERMEIREN

PATTERN HOUSE

NOORDHOEK,
CAPE TOWN,
SOUTH AFRICA

BAUHAUS

(Previous pages) Slender black-steel frames allow for large windows offering uninterrupted views across the rugged Southern Cape landscape. (Opposite and page 246) Complementing the colors of the natural environment, with its rich earth and lush vegetation, a subtle palette of warm grays and browns characterizes the home's interior spaces and furnishings.

(Above) Inside the house, whitewashed brickwork serves as a fitting backdrop to the home's minimalist interiors, some with double-height spaces. Throughout the house, carefully selected works of art, textiles, and furnishings exude a cool, midcentury vibe. (Page 243 and opposite) Viewed from the outside, the design of the house has a pleasing geometry.

Three Brick Volumes Connect Through Semi-Exposed Porches

At Casa 1101, three robust, cubic brick volumes are linked by way of exposed terraces. "One of the main goals was to achieve a close and essential relationship between the house and the garden in such a way that they both became the extension of each other," says HARQUITECTES. Despite this brief, the art-collector clients wanted walls on which to hang works from their collection, eliminating the option to have large glass panels that would typically be used to achieve this effect. Instead, it fell to the two spaces between the three structures to open the house to the front and back gardens. The first semi-exterior connecting space serves as an entrance hall, while the second, bigger space is an unconventional living room, functioning as a greenhouse in winter and a terrace in summer. These porch-like connectors stand on concrete slabs and can be closed off with folding glazed wooden doors. To contrast with the surrounding vegetation, the red, double-faced brick masonry of Casa 1101 is left in its natural color, with bricks also lining the pool to ensure an uninterrupted facade. Inside, the brickwork is painted white in places and paired with wooden window and doorframes, and concrete floors in bright, airy spaces.

HARQUITECTES

CASA 1101

SANT CUGAT DEL VALLÈS, BARCELONA, SPAIN

There is a deliberate effort to maintain a hierarchy between the interior spaces of the home and the semi-exterior connecting spaces. In the latter, the bare-brick walls and shuttered-concrete ceilings are left raw and exposed, whereas, in the former, these same surfaces are whitewashed. The effect is to ease the transition from the house to the garden.

Recycled, Reinterpreted, and Reaping the Rewards

Perched on a precipice of Australia's impressive, mountainous Great Dividing Range, Redwood House is a grand home blessed with majestic views that are ripe for exploring. Jesse Bennett Studio's commission was to refresh a 1950s home by redesigning the interior layout while maintaining the original walls. Unexpectedly, however, the walls were found to be structurally unsound, leading to a complete rebuild using the recycled materials. With a combination of modernist elements and cheeky aesthetic touches, the building is a unique interplay of concrete and masonry. The 6.5-foot- (2-meter-) high perimeter brick wall was maintained and an elevated concrete sail hovers above the home, which features a variety of brick arches ranging in height and width topped with a roof garden. The original roof tiles have been masterfully recycled on a semi-internal wall in the living room, bringing a touch of the original charm while blurring the lines between interior and exterior. Concrete, glazing, and timber join the bricks in what is an arresting reinterpretation of a midcentury home.

JESSE BENNETT STUDIO

REDWOOD HOUSE

TOOWOOMBA, QUEENSLAND, AUSTRALIA

(Previous pages) The sculptural concrete roof appears to float above the brick facades of the house. Brick also features widely throughout the design, not only in the house but also in the grounds, where it manifests as all manner of pillars, pergolas, arches, planters, and steps. (Opposite and below) An external and internal view of the wall crafted from the demolished building's roof tiles.

Trees Company for This Curvy Ghent Abode

Like the scales of an unidentified creature, a varied array of red and terra-cotta bricks—and the occasional pale-pink one—make up the curving walls of this two-story residence. The Ghent home is composed of recycled 19th-century bricks and was designed to meld with its surroundings, curving around preexisting trees. Its organic shape allows the building to be freestanding, without the need for cross walls or support beams, and the facade is punctuated by large windows that reflect the surrounding forest. Internally, the levels of the home are sectioned off in platforms, allowing some areas to have dramatic double-height ceilings. For the most part, the internal brick walls are exposed and determine the shape of each room. Where the brickwork is obscured, it has been done in such a way that the curves are accommodated, just like the nearby trees. For example, the blue tiles and bespoke wooden cabinetry of the kitchen occupy a bend in the wall, and are purposefully shaped to follow its curve.

BLAF ARCHITECTEN

GJG HOUSE

GHENT, BELGIUM

The brickwork facades employ the stretcher-bond technique, albeit with the occasional half unit here and there, since the bricks are reclaimed and likely not all whole. Bricks are also laid as headers in places—above and below windows and doors, for example, as if to reinforce their neat geometry. The building's organic shape is emphasized by the brickwork remaining exposed both inside and outside.

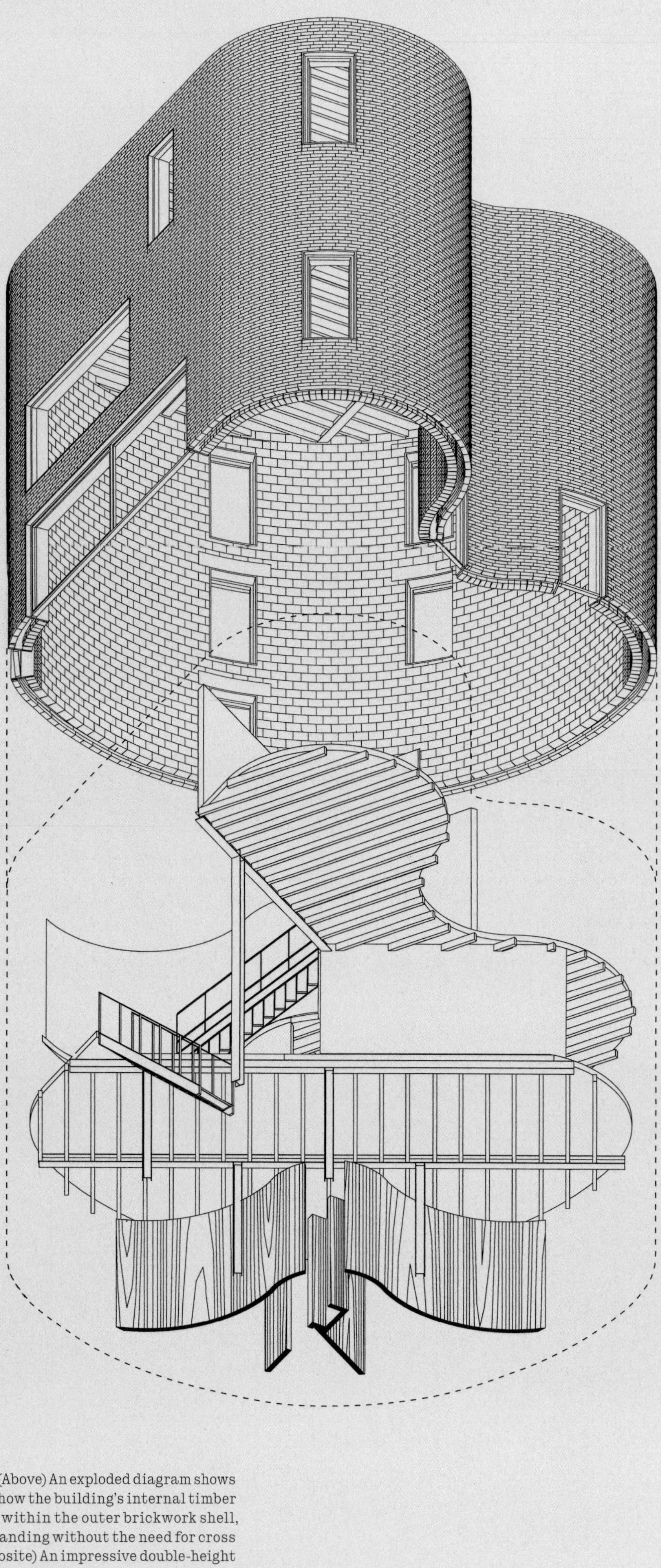

(Above) An exploded diagram shows how the building's internal timber and steel structural elements fit within the outer brickwork shell, allowing the building to be freestanding without the need for cross walls or additional supports. (Opposite) An impressive double-height living space benefits from the natural light that streams in from windows on all sides.

When observing the structure in its entirety, one can notice a gradient of blue that transitions into soft red hues at the building's base (above). The stairwells of the interior space, alternatively, are occupied by more silver and grey tones (page 270).

(Pages 266–267) The building's elegant curves see the bricks take on a warm hue in the glow of the setting sun. (Page 268, left, and below) The partially glazed parabolic arches echo the sometimes convex, sometimes concave curves of the building's facade, casting pools of light deep inside the building. Interior spaces are populated by sculptural details and furniture forms that complement the architecture.

White Bricks Pair with Black and Green in a Statement Home

Kennedy Nolan conceived an alteration and addition to this Edwardian weatherboard home, the most fundamental element of which is an entrancing circular pool, around which curved white brickwork rises. Reminiscent of white, woven, wicker furniture, the brickwork overlaps in a compellingly layered manner. Circular motifs carry throughout the house, from porthole-like windows that are peppered across the second story of the home, to circular window frames atop the arched windows surrounding the pool. Black-and-white features complement the white-painted bricks, and include black window frames, black-and-white terrazzo kitchen and poolside flooring, and white tiling in the kitchen. A powder-coated metal staircase gives a pop of forest green that finds echoes in an abstract rug in the living room. The white bricks create a subtle yet sculptural backdrop for a meticulously designed home with a minimal, yet statement color palette.

KENNEDY NOLAN

CAROLINE HOUSE

MELBOURNE, AUSTRALIA

(Above) The open-plan living space is flooded on all sides with natural light. In the dining room, a wall of timber-fronted cupboards echoes the grid-like windows that flank the green staircase and the kitchen. (Opposite) While the brickwork curves inward to embrace the circular pool on the outside, the rounded walls it creates on the inside make for dynamic and fluid interior spaces.

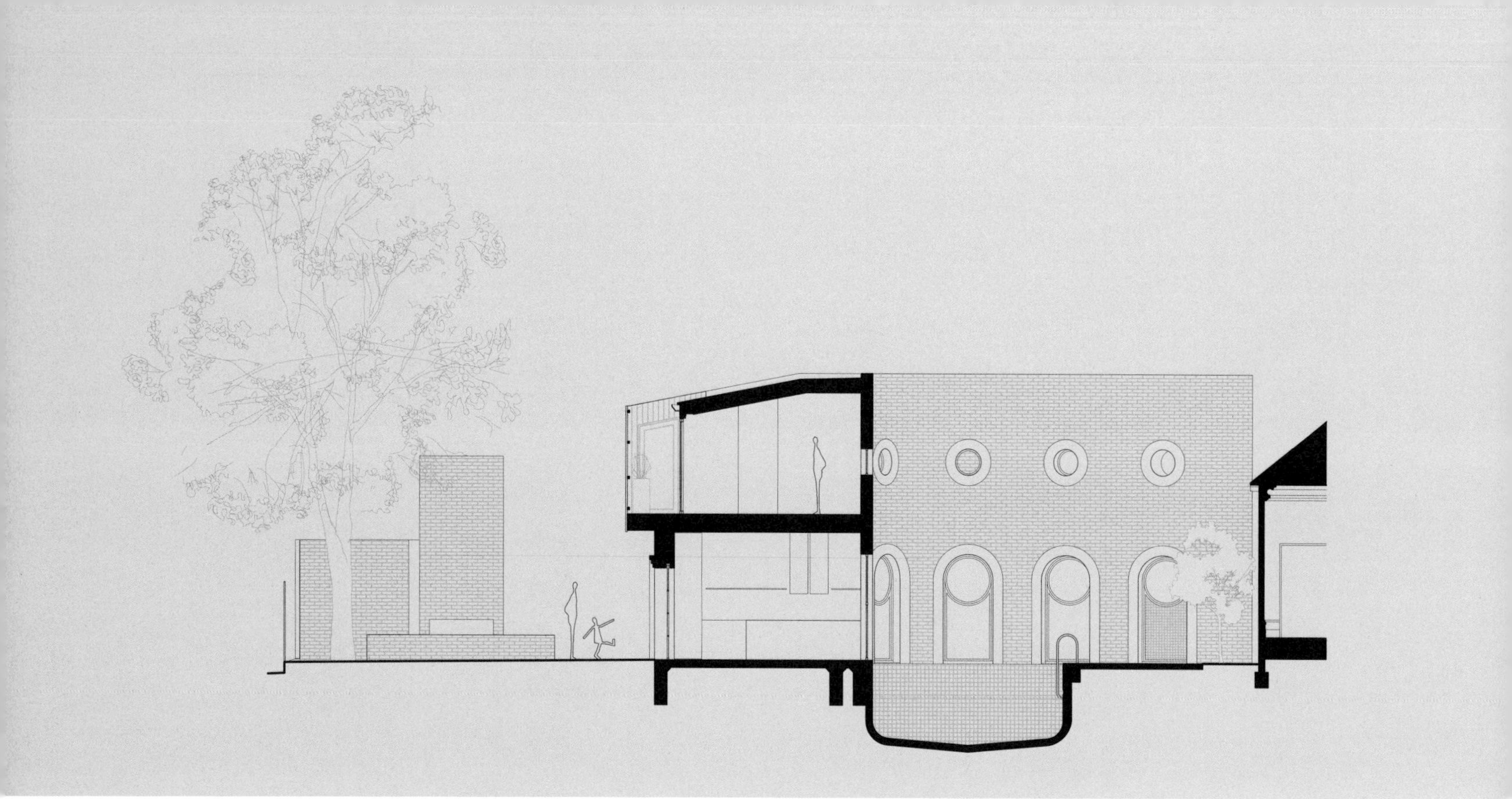

The charred timber cladding on the upper floors of the extension marks a stark contrast to the brilliant white of the brickwork below. Here, again, the circular motif is repeated, in a small window that overlooks the garden. (Opposite, bottom) A pair of Bertoia Diamond chairs cast their wonderfully geometric shadows across the black-and-white poolside terrazzo.

A Family Home with a Contemporary Aesthetic

Taking a contemporary approach with this traditional material, Ruckers Hill House, built with family life in mind, champions the brick for its durability, solidity, and craftsmanship. The home is built from light-cream Nilo Rustic bricks by LOHAS. "We chose the brick for its subtle tonal qualities and texture, which we felt would suit our design intent," says Studio Bright. The facades of the house that overlook the garden to one side and the pool on the other are punctuated with inverted arches, softening the otherwise strong, hard lines of the building. This unconventional transposal also makes the arches ideal for sitting or playing in. The motif is mirrored in indentations that run the opposite side of the pool, the brick columns creating an outdoor, room-like space reminiscent of colonnaded Roman baths. A family retreat, the house has a multi-functional interior that panders to the interests of family members while providing ideal spaces for entertaining. For example, the living area can be transformed into a performance space, with steps forming the stage. Masonry solidity underpins the design, with pavers and boulders leading from the street and into the house, and bluestone underfoot.

STUDIO BRIGHT

RUCKERS HILL HOUSE

NORTHCOTE, MELBOURNE, AUSTRALIA

(Previous pages) An open-plan kitchen is lined with light-hued timber strips. There is an area for dining as a family, as well as a breakfast bar set into a partition wall. (Opposite) The curves of the inverted brick arches in the building's external facade find echoes in the sculptural timber forms inside the house. A heavy green curtain transforms the living room into a more theatrical space.

(Opposite and previous pages) Like its historic neighbors, the Ruckers Hill House extension is built from brick, but that is where any similarities end; the design is resolutely contemporary. On the upper floors, a curved wall embraces a pair of decked rooftop courtyards, each with a border of planters. In time, the vegetation will spill over the edge of the courtyards to soften the brickwork.

MALU DE MIGUEL
MS5
Photography: Malu De Miguel
pp. 56–59

MANUEL HERZ
Maternity Paediatric Hospital
Photography: Iwan Baan/iwan.com
p. 5 top left

MARTIN SKOČEK
House V
Photography: Matej Hakár/SVK
pp. 42–49

MOHSEN KAZEMIANFARD/FUNDAMENTAL APPROACH ARCHITECT
Saadat Abad Residential Building
Photography: Courtesy of Fundamental Approach Architects/Parham Taghioff
Lead Architect: Mohsen Kazemianfard
Project Manager: Parima Jahangard
Client: Mr. Bastami
Project Construction Supervisor: Mohammadreza Bastami
Facade Construction Supervisor: Amirhossein Maleki, Parham Teimuri
pp. 118–121, 127 top

MUKA ARQUITECTURA
Casa Piedrabuena
Photography: Javier Callejas/javiercallejas.com
pp. 5 bottom, 122–125

N

NASO
Casa Martha
Photography: Maureen M. Evans/maureenme.com/@maureenme
Design Team: Patricio Aldrett, Julia Ruiz-Cabello, José Ignacio Vargas
Landscape Design: Aldaba
Furniture Design: Nomah
pp. 194 top left, 218 top left, 224–229

NIMTIM ARCHITECTS
Hive House
Photography: Megan Taylor
Structural Engineers: Blue Engineering
Main *Contractor:* TW Space Conversions Ltd
Rooflight: TW Space Conversions Ltd
Doors & Windows: ODC
Kitchen Supplier: Howdens Carcass
Bespoke Birch Ply Doors: TW Space Conversions Ltd
Worktop: Mortise
Concrete Tiles: Domus
Concrete Floor: TW Space Conversions Ltd
External Wall Lights: Mr. Resistor
Pendant Light: Hand and Eye Studio
pp. 217 top right, 230–233

O

OLAFUR ELIASSON AND SEBASTIAN BEHMANN WITH STUDIO OLAFUR ELIASSON
Fjordenhus
Artist: Olafur Eliasson
Architectural Design: Sebastian Behmann with Studio Olafur Eliasson
Project Architect: Caspar Teichgräber
Local Architect: Lundgaard & Tranberg Architecture
Landscape Architect: Vogt Landscape Ltd.
Photography: Anders Sune Berg
Client: KIRK KAPITAL A/S
pp. 266–271

P

PETER BEHRENS
Hoechst Administration Building
Photography: Arcaid Images/Alamy Stock Photo (**p. 138 bottom left & bottom right**), Courtesy of Infraserv GmbH & Co. Höchst KG (**p. 139**)

PHILIP WEBB AND WILLIAM MORRIS
Red House
Photography: Laurence Mackman/Alamy Stock Photo
pp. 64–65

R

REIULF RAMSTAD ARKITEKTER
Kornets Hus
Photography: Reiulf Ramstad Arkitekter
pp. 144–147

S

STATE OF KIN
Brick House
Photography: Jack Lovel
pp. 131 top, 184–189, 217 middle right

STONECYCLING
stonecycling.com
Photography: StoneCycling (**pp. 128 top right, 192 top right, 195 middle right**), Dim Balsem (**p. 128 bottom left**), Studio Amy V/D Horst (**p. 131 middle right**), Nienke Krook (**pp. 192 bottom left, 193 top right, 194 bottom left**)

STUDIOATA
Una Finestra sulle Langhe
Photography: Beppe Giardino
Group Leader: Studioata
Architecture: Studioata
Structure: Ing. Michele De Rossi
Consultant for Environmental Sustainability: Ing. Davide Ambrosio
Constructor: Aimo Costruzioni s.r.l. – Mondovì (CN)
Facing Bricks: Alberto Cavallera
Fixtures: Automation Doors s.r.l. – Grimaldi serramenti
Iron Works: ESSE-CI s.r.l.
Supplier Bricks: Terreal Italia s.r.l.
pp. 32–35

STUDIO BRIGHT
Clinker Brick House
Photography: Rory Gardiner
Project Team: Melissa Bright, Robert McIntyre, Maia Close, Emily Watson
Builder: CBD Contracting Group
Engineer Consultants: Meyer Consulting
Contracting Company: AH Brick and Block
pp. 36–41

Garden Wall House
Photography: Sean Fennessy
Project Team: Melissa Bright, Robert McIntyre, Emily Watson, Todd de Hoog
Builder: Build2
Building Surveyor: BSGM
Structural Engineer: Hive Engineering
Landscape Consultant: Eckersley Garden Architecture
pp. 50–51

Perimeter House
Photography: Peter Bennetts
Project Team: Melissa Bright, Robert McIntyre, Emily Watson, Todd de Hoog, Grace McKellar, Maia Close, Bruce Rowe, Pei She Lee
Builder: Basis Builders
Engineer: Hive Engineering
Building Surveyor: Fotia Group
pp. 148–153

Ruckers Hill House
Photography: Courtesy of Studio Bright/Rory Gardiner
Project Team: Melissa Bright, Robert McIntyre, Todd de Hoog, Emily Watson, Pei She Lee, Maia Close, Rachel Freeman
Builder: 4AD Construction
Engineer: Meyer Consulting
Landscape Design: TNLA and Studio Bright
Landscape Install: MJR Landscape
Contracting Company: Robin Gifford, John Dafnis and Richard Baigent
pp. 278–285

STUDIO ZHU-PEI
Jingdezhen Imperial Kiln Museum
Photography: Courtesy of Studio Zhu-Pei
pp. 72, 75 bottom

T

TALLER DE ARQUITECTURA MAURICIO ROCHA + GABRIELA CARRILLO
Iturbide Studio
Photography: Rafael Gamo/rafaelgamo.com
pp. 131 bottom left, 214, 216 top right, 217 bottom

TIKARI WORKS
The Rye
Photography: Jack Hobhouse
Shingle Manufacturer: Petersen Tegl
SubContractor: Eurban CLT
Manufacturer: Stora Enso
pp. 22–25, 75 middle left

TOSHIHIRO OKI
Bellport House
Photography: Dean Kaufman
Structural and Mechanical Engineer: Condon Engineering
Brick: Petersen Tegl
pp. 160–165

TRAANSPACE
The Brick Connection
Photography: Umang Shah
Architect: TRAANSPACE
Principal Architect: Urvi Shah
Client: Pankaj Lunawat & Dipika Lunawat
pp. 178–183, 218 top right

W

WALLMAKERS
Pirouette House
Photography: Jino Sam
Design Team: Oshin Mariam Varughese, J.M.Srivarshini, Gayatri Maithani, Swathi Raj, Keerthi Kausalya, Shiuly Roy, Neeraj S. Murali, Dhawal Dasari
Engineering: Adcons Infrastructure Pvt Ltd
Fabrication: Kunjumon James and team/J.K. steels
Carpenters: Sarath Prasad and team/Shivadas
Masons: Ezhil, Deepu
pp. 77 top, 78–83, 217 top left, 219 bottom left & top

WANG SHU/AMATEUR ARCHITECTURE STUDIO
Fuyang Cultural Complex
Photography: Iwan Baan/iwan.com
pp. 190–191, 195 top

WILLEM MARINUS DUDOK
Hilversum Town Hall
Photography: Tasfoto/Alamy Stock Photo (**pp. 136 top, 137**), Ger Beekes/Alamy Stock Photo (**136 bottom**)

WILL GAMBLE ARCHITECTS
The Parchment Works
Photography: Johan Dehlin
Aluminium Glazing: Maxlight
Corten Cladding: Lindsey Fabrication & Engineering
Oak Flooring: Reeve Wood
Joinery: TD Furniture
Stone Floor: Mandarin Stone
pp. 66–71, 77 bottom left, 193 middle right

Additional Credits

J. Enrique Molina/Alamy Stock Photo (**p. 12**), Phil Crean/Alamy Stock Photo (**p. 13 top**), Porky Pies Photography/Alamy Stock Photo (**p. 14 top**), Horst Friedrichs/Alamy Stock Photo (**p. 14 bottom**), B.O'Kane/Alamy Stock Photo (**p. 15 top left**), Giuseppe Spartà/Alamy Stock Photo (**p. 15 top right**), Petr Svarc/Alamy Stock Photo (**p. 15 middle right**), Ros Drinkwater/Alamy Stock Photo (**p. 15 bottom right**), Andriy Shevchenko/Alamy Stock Photo (**p. 16 top left**), Kabataan/Alamy Stock Photo (**p. 16 top right**), Andreas Altenburger/Alamy Stock Photo (**p. 16 bottom left**), Bildagentur-online/Exss/Alamy Stock Photo (**p. 17 top**), Findlay/Alamy Stock Photo (**p. 17 middle right**), Artem Konovalov/Alamy Stock Photo (**p. 17 bottom left**), Arcaid Images/Alamy Stock Photo (**pp. 194 top right, 195 bottom left**), Edmund Sumner-VIEW/Alamy Stock Photo (**p. 218 bottom left**)

Brick by Brick

Architecture and Interiors Built with Bricks

This book was conceived, edited, and designed by gestalten.

Edited by Robert Klanten and Andrea Servert

Introduction by Natalia Torija
Feature texts by Natalia Torija: pp. 72–77, 190–195, and 214–219, Alisa Kotmair: pp. 12–17, and 126–131
Project texts and Glossary by Laura Box
Captions by Anna Southgate

Editorial Management by Anastasia Buryak

Design, layout, and cover by Stefan Morgner

Photo Editor: Madeleine Dudley-Yates

Illustrations: Kate Evans

Typeface: Cucina by Lucas Le Bihan

Cover image by Reiulf Ramstad Arkitekter

Backcover: Studioata, photo by Beppe Giardino (top right); Wallmakers, photo by Jino Sam (middle left); Batay-Csorba, photo by Doublespace Photography (middle right); GRAFT, photo by Noam Rosenthal / Trockland Management GmbH (bottom right)

Printed by Gutenberg Beuys Feindruckerei GmbH, Langenhagen
Made in Germany

Published by gestalten, Berlin 2022
ISBN 978-3-96704-001-2

For more information, and to order books, please visit www.gestalten.com

Bibliographic information published by the Deutsche Nationalbibliothek. The Deutsche Nationalbibliothek lists this publication in the Deutsche Nationalbibliografie; detailed bibliographic data is available online at www.dnb.de

This book was printed on paper certified according to the standards of the FSC®.

MIX
Paper from responsible sources
FSC® C009051